DANDELION HUNTER
Foraging the Urban Wilderness

REBECCA LERNER

LYONS PRESS
Guilford, Connecticut
An imprint of Globe Pequot Press

To buy books in quantity for corporate use
or incentives, call **(800) 962-0973**
or e-mail **premiums@GlobePequot.com.**

Lyons Press is an imprint of Globe Pequot Press.

Project Editor: David Legere
Text Design: Sheryl P. Kober
Layout Artist: Sue Murray

Library of Congress Cataloging-in-Publication Data is available on file.

ISBN 978-0-7627-8062-4

Printed in the United States of America
10 9 8 7 6 5 4 3 2 1

The information in this book is not intended to diagnose, treat, cure, or prevent any disease. The author does not dispense medical advice or prescribe
the use of any substance as a form of treatment for any medical ailment,
either directly or indirectly. The intent of this author is only to offer information of a general nature, based on her own experiences and the teachings
of various herbal traditions. In the event you use information in this book
for yourself, the author and the publisher assume no responsibility for your
actions.

For the plants, my friends and teachers

CONTENTS

Part Four: I Think I Love You

AUTHOR'S NOTE

This is a work of nonfiction. The dialogue was digitally recorded, and, when that was not possible—such as when conversations took place before I planned on writing about them—written from memory to the best of my ability and then later confirmed with the other parties involved.

Some of the people described herein have their last names listed; this is because they consented to that. If they wanted more privacy, I refer to them by first name only.

I mention the Latin names of some plants discussed herein in order to aid in specificity, as common names may vary.

FOREWORD

This book is set in the rainy Pacific Northwest, in the lush, green city of Portland, Oregon. It follows my adventures as an urban forager—a person who picks wild plants from the sidewalks, parks, alleyways, and other common spaces of a metropolis—as I challenge myself to survive on wild food, make my own medicine, and learn to see nature in a new way.

Every wild plant has a gift to offer. Plants are food and medicine, paint pigments, twine, soap, incense, tinder, insulation, beauty products—and the list goes on, because before there was "an app for that," there was a plant for that.

PART ONE:

What to Eat at the End of the World

1
Wild Girl

The stranger walked across her front lawn to meet me at dusk. She waded through a wall of weeds as high as her hips, parting the sea of greens like a post-modern Moses.

"Hi," I said, standing on her driveway. "I'm your neighbor, and I'd like to eat your weeds."

Though I lived just a few blocks away, we had never met before. Her house was set behind a frayed wooden fence at the corner of a busy intersection with a stoplight. It was odd-looking: small and squat and made of concrete, with just a short square window, like a prison. I thought it was a garage until I looked more closely and noticed an address spray-painted over the door.

"What's that?" she said, looking at me with a furrowed brow.

"Well, I'm doing this survival challenge where I'm only eating wild food that I forage in Portland for a week, and this is the first day, and I haven't been able to find anything good yet. Can I eat your weeds?"

The rules I had set for myself were simple. For seven days, my meals would come from sidewalk strips and alleyways and public parks and wherever else I could forage wild plants around the city. My preference was to stay within a couple miles of my apartment—walking distance, really— but the permissible territory would encompass the general metro area. There would be no gleaning from community gardens, no Dumpster diving outside grocery stores, and certainly nothing purchased. Before I began, I cleaned out my cabinets and my fridge, removing the accoutrements of my vegetarian[1] diet—hummus, tofu, nut milk, avocados— and passing them off to friends and neighbors.

⁂

Conventionally, as seen on TV, a wilderness survival challenge is when a helicopter drops a grizzled, sun-beaten man with military training and a bandanna into an unfamiliar habitat to struggle for his life in dangerous conditions that will test his courage, perhaps in the Alaskan tundra in the dead of winter, or maybe in the Kalahari desert without

---

1. I went vegetarian when I was sixteen after I watched a PETA video on factory farming. I was appalled at the cruelty I saw and disturbed that an entire industry profits by enslaving animals from birth to death, forcing many of them to spend their entire lives indoors in warehouses, isolated from their parents and children, in uncomfortable and unsanitary conditions. I decided not to eat meat anymore because I didn't want to cause unnecessary suffering. I had no problem with the Kalahari bushmen who stalk warthogs through the desert with spears because they need to eat them.

water, or some other exotic location as far from civilization as possible. My version of this adventure was very different. I was supposing that the wilderness is everywhere in our midst. In a sense, it is—think of all the human animals running around. No matter how many chemicals we invent or how advanced our electronic gadgets become, our flesh remains as biodegradable as dirt and leaves. Like birds and bunnies and bears, we are the product of millions of years of evolution on this planet. The city is just another kind of habitat. Even though we walk on synthetic carpets and talk to each other with electronic machines, and even though the outdoors can seem a mere vestibule between home and work, or home and the supermarket, when we deepen our gaze on these short trips through the wilderness, we are bound to find a deeper dimension.

My neighbor's yard sprawled for a good half-acre. To her eye it must have looked like an unruly mess, but to me it was most appealing in its current state: a veritable u-pick farm blooming with feral food. I saw bright yellow dandelion blossoms, *Taraxacum officinale*, and the fuschia flowers of red clover, *Trifolium pratense*, and sheep sorrel, *Rumex acetosella*, a grassy-looking herb with rust-colored tips and leaves that, when turned sideways, are shaped like the profile view of a sheep's head, ears and all. It is the most pleasant tasting of the three, tart and citrusy. I picked a leaf and ate it, and then I handed one to her.

"Hey," she said, chewing. "That's not bad."

From a botanical perspective, there is no such thing as a weed; the word means nothing more than a plant that's growing where some human thinks it shouldn't. More often than not, the plants we call weeds are food. The familiar dandelion is native to the Mediterranean, where it is an ingredient in traditional Italian dishes. Purslane, *Portulaca oleracea*, a delicious oily plant fond of growing in sidewalk cracks, is cuisine in Africa and China.

Despite their abundance, it wasn't as easy to find a good weed as I thought it would be. The first thing I did was walk the ins and outs of a twenty-block radius around my apartment looking for plants to eat. I spent a long time examining the sidewalks of Alberta Street, the mile-long stretch of art galleries and cafes at the heart of the neighborhood. It was hip but still rough around the edges, with unpaved side streets and occasional gang shootings on the periphery late at night. Some say the area recalls Greenwich Village in its heyday, except that the buildings on Alberta Street are only one or two stories high, and they're painted bright colors like in the Caribbean. Portland pulses with the slow, laid-back pace for which the West Coast is known. You see men carrying teddy bears in baby wraps across their chests. You see bicyclists wearing Viking horns and long capes fluttering in the wind.

A decade earlier this had been a working-class black neighborhood. The more recent transplants are white, tattooed people in their twenties and thirties moving in from across the country. More than a few are circus folk who ride unicycles down the street. My own contribution to the ambience was a cherry red Mohawk that prompted passersby to inquire which band I was the front woman for. "None," I'd say. "I just look badass."

After hours scanning the sidewalks for weeds, I came to the disappointing realization that they were essentially barren, more like a living history museum of forgotten food crops from the Victorian era than the Wonka Land I had been expecting. Rendered inedible by circumstance, edible plants seemed to grow only in three toxic conditions: mingling with dog turds, against a painted wall, or covered in dust from the exhaust fumes of passing cars. Look, but don't touch. Or touch, but don't eat. So my neighbor's lawn was a huge score. Except for one little issue.

"My landlord said I have to mow all of this by tonight," she told me. "You got here just in time."

The sun was setting. I pulled weeds by the handful and raced back to my apartment to make dinner.

Portland has the kind of features real estate agents love to boast about: Snow-covered volcanoes rise to the clouds in the distance, old-growth rain forests ring the metropolis, and gardens are productive, enjoying long growing seasons with plenty of precipitation. But the city also has something a little less charming: impending doom. On a slow news day, this is the sort of thing you might read in one of the local weeklies: "In the reasonably near future, perhaps within our lifetimes and quite possibly as soon as tomorrow, an earthquake will strike Portland with roughly the same force felt this month in Port-au-Prince. But while the January 12 Haitian quake lasted less than forty seconds, the shaking in Portland will continue for at least four minutes. Portland will feel a quake with a strength, duration, and destruction never before experienced in the developed Western world." That is the beginning of an article that ran in the *Willamette Week* newspaper in January 2010. It continues:

"Underground gas, power, and water lines will be pulverized. The soil beneath the Portland International Airport will temporarily turn to soup . . . This . . . is the scientific consensus on what will happen here sooner or later. And the latest data suggest it may in fact be sooner . . . The latest studies of undersea landslide debris, released last spring by Oregon State University geologist Chris Goldfinger, suggest a Cascadia subduction zone quake happens every 300 to 350 years. The last one occurred 310 years ago yesterday."

The thing about living in a place that could crack at any given moment is that you get to thinking about survival situations in a more serious way than people who read zombie novels in, say, Pennsylvania. You get to thinking about them kind of often, actually. Even people who are not living on a fault line can choose their own adventure from a dazzling array of options: hurricanes and tsunamis, infectious disease, volcanoes, nuclear war, solar storms, asteroids, economic collapse, and so forth. Any of the above could short electricity and disrupt the transportation of farm-raised foods to grocery stores, leaving us to suddenly fend for ourselves off the grid. When water ceases to flow through garden hoses, crops will wilt, but wild plants will be thriving as much as ever.

I am an apartment dweller. I have no land to call my own. A test run at foraging seemed as good a form of apocalypse insurance as any.

I was optimistic that I could succeed. For one thing, I knew that foraging is a time-tested subsistence strategy with a track record of sustainability. Humans lived as hunter-gatherers for 95 percent of the two hundred thousand years we have existed on Earth as *Homo sapiens*. Or, if we trace humanity back 2.4 million years to the emergence of *Homo habilis*, then people have been foraging 99 percent of the time. No matter where we come from or what our ethnicity may be, we all have hunter-gatherer DNA. We all have ancestors who foraged for a living.

This idea of living off wild food in a city would be unique only in terms of its era. For more than ten thousand years, the valley at the confluence of the Columbia and Willamette Rivers supported one of the densest populations of hunter-gatherers in North America. Here, in the land now known as Portland, the Clackamas Chinook people—including the Wacanessi'si and Multnomah tribes, and their ancestors—sustained themselves exclusively on wild food. They feasted on salmon, lamprey eel, elk, and deer, and many kinds of plants, especially acorns from the Oregon white oak, *Quercus garryana*; camas bulbs, *Camassia quamash;* a root called wapato, *Sagittaria latifolia*; huckleberry, *Vaccinum* spp.; and salal berry, *Gaultheria shallon*.[2] If they could live off wild food here year-round, then surely I could forage for a week in the same place in late May 2009.

Right?

$$\text{❦}$$

I poured the bag full of weeds into a colander in my kitchen sink. The green plantain leaves mixed with the yellow dandelions and purple clover blossoms and the rusty-colored sorrel tops as they all tumbled into the bowl. I rinsed them under the faucet and shook them dry, then tore them to pieces to make a big salad. There was no dressing, as bottles of bleu cheese do not sprout in the wild. I set the table, then separated out some of the plantain and dandelion leaves and put them in a pot on the stove to steam as a main course.

I had tasted these wild plants raw on the street many times, but this was my first time making a meal out of them. It was a big moment. I sat down at my kitchen table and took the first bite. The sugary clover flowers tasted good against the citrusy flavor of the sheep sorrel. But then the leaves and stems became chewy and dry in my mouth, an unpleasant texture that suggested I was eating lawnmower clippings.

2. Life took a dramatic turn when white settlers and missionaries arrived in the 1840s, settling down at the last stop on the Oregon Trail and bringing their domesticated crops, weeds, diseases, and farming practices with them. When smallpox, malaria, typhoid, and measles killed more than 90 percent of the indigenous population, white settlers took control of the Willamette Valley, chopping down trees and carving the land into rectangles. People called it Stumptown, a nickname Portland still carries today.

Acid pooled behind my tongue and I felt nauseous. My stomach tightened. Hungry as I was, I just couldn't stand to take another bite.[3]

I held out hope for the main course. I'd read in a field guide that plantain leaves taste "like Swiss chard," and I knew that pilgrims intentionally brought dandelion on the *Mayflower* to grow as food. Nutritional analyses have found dandelion rich in vitamin E, iron, calcium, and potassium.

As I spooned the steamed plantain and dandelion greens onto my plate, I noticed that they had wilted like spinach with that same rich, dark green color. I stabbed the leaves with my fork and put them eagerly into my mouth. In went a blast of bitterness. I kept chewing, and the thick veins of the plantain leaves stuck in my teeth like dental floss. Here was a new experience: to feel both hungry and uninterested in food at the same time. The Swiss chard claim was clearly bunk.[4] It wasn't until later that I learned that the older a plant gets, the more bitter its leaves become. I must have eaten some curmudgeons.

The thing about hunger is it changes shape. On the first day it nagged at me with a dull ache. On the second it grew more acute, a neon sign flashing EAT.

---

3. It was not until three years later that I read that red clover can cause bloating and upset stomach in some people. "The Bloat" may have killed some American Indians who were forced to subsist on this plant, according to field guide author Steve Brill.

4. Some field guides appear to be compendiums of rumors. The better ones are written by authors who have personal experience with foraging. See the appendix for recommended titles.

My breakfast on the second day was a tea made of pineapple weed, *Matricaria matricarioides,* also known as wild chamomile, plucked from a chain-link fence a few blocks from my apartment. Then I went looking for food at Lewis and Clark State Park, a wilderness area near the Columbia Gorge along the Sandy River. I knew how to identify about two dozen species of edible wild plants, but in case I encountered some unfamiliar ones, I asked my friend Emily Porter to accompany me and save me from winning a Darwin Award.[5]

Emily is a self-described "plant genius" who once worked as a botanist for the US Forest Service after teaching herself with stacks of field guides and books on herbs. We met when I came to a class on edible wild plants she was teaching at a local wilderness survival school in a drafty, dimly lit warehouse on the east side of town. It was just Emily and I and a handful of skinny white dudes in their twenties with scruffy hipster beards.

Emily perched on the edge of a wooden table and passed out specimens she'd harvested from the park across the street. "This one is lemon balm, *Melissa officinalis,*" she said softly, averting her eyes as she passed it around. She picked up a reference book and read aloud from it, explaining to us that the plant can be dried and made into a tea with antianxiety effects, and then she folded her arms and looked toward the floor instead of at us.

5. The Darwin Awards are given posthumously to people who die from stupidity, in recognition of the altruism they display in removing themselves from the gene pool.

Emily is pretty. She has a sweet face with glossy brown hair and a tall, sleek build, like a fashion model. She is also pretty unusual, in that she has a muted affect and an odd way of speaking. Her sentences have long pauses in the middle of them, and her replies to questions can sometimes take minutes to emerge. This requires some getting used to, but I like eccentric people.[6] Maybe my talkative nature complemented her reticence, or maybe it was just our shared interest in eating urban wild plants that brought us together, but Emily and I became friends pretty quickly.

The two of us would go for walks around town with our eyes glued to the ground, strolling around Portland, just hanging out, and I would point to any given green creature and say, "Hey, Emily, what's that?" And she would know. She would have an answer for me, and it would be amazing. One time her answer was, "Plantain, *Plantago major*." And I said, "Well, how do you know?" And she pointed out the hairless texture of the leaves and the coarse, stringy, parallel veins on the underside, and the distinctive structure of the flower, which looks like a skinny brown microphone. "What can you do with it?" I asked. She told me I could eat the leaves, or chew them up and spit them on a bug bite to stop the itching, or spit it on a splinter to draw it out, and that I could drink the seeds in a tea if I needed a laxative, too.

I admired that she could see things nobody else knew were even there. It was like she had superpowers, something akin to X-ray vision. She could peer into what I

---

6. "Do I qualify as eccentric?" I asked a friend one day, wondering if it takes one to know one. He said, "Sure, I've got the paperwork right here."

thought was a mass of green foliage and see medicine. It took me a while to acquire something resembling that. It happened a little at a time. At first I thought all plants looked alike. They tend to be green, have leaves, have stalks, and live on the ground. Some are taller than others, but at first glance there isn't much difference between them, especially if they're not flowering. Trying to sort out their subtleties seemed like attempting one of those "spot-the-difference" photo puzzles. "How can you tell plants apart?" I'd ask Emily. "How can you be sure the one you're about to eat isn't something poisonous?"

Poison hemlock and wild carrot look a lot alike, and if I mistook the demure carrot for its cousin, I would die, just like Socrates did after eating it. The trick, Emily taught me, is that we get to use more than just our eyeballs to know about the world. Looking at those two plants, we might not be able to tell them apart, but if we touched the stems, we could distinguish them instantly. Carrot, *Daucus carota,* is also known as Queen Anne's lace, and Emily has a little story she likes to tell about it: "Queen Anne forgot to shave her legs," she says. The carrot stem is very hairy, stubbly even, while the stem of poison hemlock is silky smooth. Poison hemlock sometimes leaves a powdery white film on your fingers, too. So we get to use our other senses—they're no longer ornamental.

In late spring, I noticed this one particular plant all over the city. It was about half a foot tall with finely dissected leaves and round yellow flowers that, lacking petals, reminded me of pencil erasers. It seemed that wherever I went for a few weeks, I would see its bright yellow flowers there. It popped up in gravel footpaths, along sidewalk strips, and behind chain-link fences. I was dying to know its name. If I could know its name, then I could know what present it had to offer me. Every time I learn a new plant, the world expands.

The feeling was much like that nagging one you get when you're at a party and someone says hello to you, and she looks vaguely familiar, but you don't know how you know her, and it seems like she knows who you are, and you can't ask her name because that might hurt her feelings and make you look like kind of an ass. The moment you get away, you tap the host on the shoulder and eagerly whisper, "Who *is* that person?" You're just dying to know, and if the host doesn't know, then you're consumed with the mystery, asking all the partygoers until you find out. It's like that with new plants, for me.

One day I asked Emily about it. "Oh, that's pineapple weed," she said. "You can tell by the smell." I got down on my hands and knees and stuck my nose right up to the flower and inhaled, and that's when a fruity, tropical scent wafted into my nose. When I touched the flower, it grew even stronger, because pineapple weed is a scratch-and-sniff.

੪

It was a hot day when Emily and I went to roam the hiking path under bigleaf maple, *Acer macrophyllum,* and cottonwood trees, *Populus balsamiferus,* and found very little food. We saw a lot of barren snowberry bushes, *Symphoricarpos albus,* which have white berries in the winter that can be used for soap but are not edible. The wooded area opened into a sun-drenched riparian meadow. There along the edges we found some wild rose, *Rosa nutkana,* which doesn't look like the ornamental kind—it has five pink petals and a bright yellow center. I ate a few rose blossoms. We also found ground ivy, *Glecoma hederacea,* a pungent mint suitable for tea, and some very good-tasting salad greens in the form of miner's lettuce, *Claytonia perfoliata,* and chickweed, *Stellaria media.* I was most excited at the prospect of digging up the few wild carrot roots we came across, but they had very little to offer calorically. They were shorter and thinner than my pinky.

I had assumed that a forest full of plants would have a lot of food in it. But after five hours of concerted effort, we had collected hardly anything, only handfuls of salad greens and tea herbs. I felt disappointed and frustrated, and I was starting to get grumpy. I began to resign myself to another day of famine until, on the way back to the parking lot, Emily spotted a large stand of stinging nettle a short distance off the path. This was a score. Stinging nettle, *Urtica dioica,* is one of the most nourishing plants you can find. It grows in partial shade in moist forest habitats across the continent. It tastes a bit like spinach and is packed with iron, calcium, potassium, vitamins A, C, and D, and has gobs of essential fatty acids. Some reports say it may be up to 25 percent protein. Nettle has a humid, green-tea-like smell to it that wafts several feet away, and in appearance it resembles a mint plant, with square stems and serrated leaves that grow opposite each other, except that nettle is armed with little stinging hairs. Hikers who brush past it come away feeling like they've had a run-in with angry ants—both the insects and the plant inject you with formic acid, leaving a sting that lingers for hours in the form of tingling bumps. Those willing to harvest it, though, will find that stinging nettle has a multitude of uses. Fibers in the outer layer of the stem make sturdy cordage, and when you brew the leaves as a tea, you will have an astringent hair rinse to treat dandruff. You can also steep the aboveground portions of the plant in alcohol in a glass jar for weeks to make an extract that, when taken regularly, treats allergies.

The tricky part is getting the plant. Because of all the stingers, a lot of people wear gloves when they harvest. I didn't have any. There were more complications. The plants were already flowering, which is not an ideal time to eat because the texture becomes tougher and drier. What's more, the patch was six feet tall; I am five foot five inches. And I was wearing a sleeveless shirt.

I got up on my tippy-toes and delicately tilted a pair of scissors toward the leaves while attempting to keep my wrists from touching them. My plan was to snip the tops and catch them in a paper grocery bag I held open with my other hand. Trimming just the top of nettle is a way to avoid killing the plant—it's like giving it a haircut. Plus, the top leaves are usually the youngest ones, and the youngest are usually the most tender. At first I thought my method was working well, but just as I started feeling confident, those stinging hairs zapped me a few times, sending a jolt of pain and adrenaline coursing through my veins. It was less painful than a bee sting, but it still smarted for hours.

So that I could have something other than just nettle to eat that day, Emily suggested we stop by a park with a different ecology on the way home. We chose Forest Park, the largest forested natural area within the city limits of Portland and in the whole United States. It has five thousand acres of tall Douglas-fir, *Pseudotsuga menziesii,* Western red cedar, *Thuja plicata,* and red alder, *Alnus rubra,* interspersed with elderberry, *Sambucus racemosa,* hazelnut, *Corylus cornuta,* and red huckleberry, *Vaccinium parvifolium.* The latter three shrubs would have given us nuts and berries later in the year, but at this time, late May, we had little to choose from but weeds.

One of the largest and most prolific was burdock, *Arctium minus,* which has large, fuzzy, ruffled leaves shaped like elephant ears and attached to smooth, thick purple stalks that grow in a rosette shape from the root. The plant lives for two or three years. We were glad to find the first-year variety, because once the burdock plant sends up a tall stalk, the roots become too woody to eat, and they can grow as deep as three feet, making them very difficult to dig up even if you wanted to. Emily and I took turns getting at the roots, using a hand trowel at the side of a trail and hoping no one was watching.

§

At home, I rinsed the burdock and peeled away the rough brown outer bark to reveal starchy, cream-colored root meat, then stuck it in the oven to bake. We had gotten about a dozen roots, each about the thickness and length of a shoe-string French fry. Scattered on the hot tray, they reminded me of wood chips. It was not much in the way of food, but after the failed salad the day before and little else since, it seemed like a hard-earned feast.

I poured the nettle into a pot of water on the stove and turned up the heat. That was one way to deactivate the stingers—cooking the plant in hot water. Other ways to do it are by crushing the leaves or shredding them in a food processor. Drying them works, too.

The boiled nettle stems and leaves were so old that they were unpleasant to eat, so I decided just to drink the oily broth instead. It reminded me of vegetable stock. It was so good that I had to tell someone, so I knocked on my neighbor's door. We weren't friends, exactly, but we did share an Internet connection. He lived across the hall.

"You have to try this," I told him. "It's amazing!" He eyed the bowl of golden liquid with suspicion, then took a tiny sip from the spoon and gave me a polite thumbs-up. "Not bad," he said, and then excused himself.

I began the third day with a breakfast tea of needles from pine trees, *Pinus ponderosa,* gathered from the landscaping in front of my apartment complex. I knew which species it was because it had a cluster of three needles and because Emily had taught me that when you stick your nose in deeply furrowed ponderosa bark, it smells faintly of vanilla. I added wild rose blossoms and aboveground parts of ground ivy that I had picked with Emily the day before, along with some pineapple weed I found along a sidewalk on Alberta. I also snacked on some purslane that I found growing in a raised planter outside of a retail business. Like nettle, it is rich in fatty acids. It crawls along the soil with paddle-shaped leaves and rubbery pink stems. With an oily texture and a crisp, faintly lemony flavor, it is one of the best edible weeds there is.

For lunch I made stinging nettle broth again, then went back to Lewis and Clark State Park, this time to search for mushrooms with an acquaintance who was a professional mushroom hunter, supplying gourmet chefs with morels for profit. Though we had found an abundance of delectable morels just a couple of weeks prior, he said he didn't expect to find any now. I didn't believe him that so many mushrooms could vanish in a matter of days, but as it turned out, he was right. Hours of wandering, and we came out empty-handed.

I needed food, so I went back to Forest Park and had slightly better luck. I dug up more burdock root and plucked some cleavers, *Galium aparine*, also known as bedstraw, which are named for their habit of clinging to your clothing with little clasps they have along their stem and leaves. The leaves are funny-looking, splayed out like stars on a string. They are edible, but their texture makes them a little bit tricky to chew, so I took them home, chopped them up, and stuck them in a cheesecloth bag to make a cold tea that tastes like cucumber water.

That evening, as the sun sank past the trees outside, I sat down on my couch feeling very, very tired. I had spent more than eight hours searching for food. Though I had hardly taken in any calories, I was surprised to find that my stomach did not ache any longer. I now thought of food only as fuel to enable my physical activity. With enough exhaustion I forgot my hunger, and like a bat fleeing daybreak, it retreated.

ॐ

If I hadn't craved a tofu sandwich a few months earlier, I might never have been in this situation. I remember that day very well. I bought the sandwich at a local grocery store and then I sat down to eat it in the cafe section, at one of those countertops set right in front of the windows looking out onto the street, when this pale string bean of a man with a mop of white hair plopped down a little too close in the seat next to me and started talking to me as if we knew each other, going on about his life and his work as an oil-industry analyst turned environmental activist. He seemed like a nice person, a decent person, a person I might be ideologically aligned with, but I wasn't in the mood for company, especially not the kind provided by a stranger. Who did he think he was, intruding on my solitude? I thought he was a little weird, a little forward, a little overly friendly. I was considering whether to get up and leave, but then he mentioned that he lived on a sailboat, and I started thinking that maybe I would listen a little longer. Hey, this guy was kind of interesting. Hey, maybe this was not so bad for lunchtime entertainment—a monologue, just like listening to the radio. When he told me he was the editor and publisher of an online magazine, then he had my full attention.

"I'm a journalist," I said, handing him my card. "I have a blog."

I was new in town. I had been a newspaper reporter in New Jersey and upstate New York and moved here because I wanted to live on the West Coast. When I got here I hardly knew anyone,and it took nearly a month before I found a cheap enough place to live that I could stop sleeping in my car. I was eager for writing gigs, but I could hardly get editors to respond to my e-mails at the time. It seemed you had to know someone. I was channeling my latent reporting skills into a blog I called First Ways, where I catalogued the edible wild plants I was learning about in books and from friends. I posted my photographs of them, researched their historical uses in field guides and ethnobotanical encyclopedias, and experimented in trying them out for myself. Blogging helped me retain what I was learning and share it with others at the same time. I liked the feeling of uncovering long-buried secrets. It was like investigative reporting, except cheerful.

The stranger turned his laptop to show me his website. The banner said Culture Change, and he said its mission was to warn the world that The End of Oil Is Near and Economic Collapse Is, Too. It will happen any day now, he said, and his goal is to establish a sustainable infrastructure for transporting food and other essential goods in advance of an emergency. His pet project, Sail Transport Network, shipped local produce by sailboat and bicycle instead of by car.

I thought he seemed alarmist, but also kind of visionary: Petroleum is a limited resource, and everyone knows industrial civilization is unsustainable. We are in the midst of the sixth greatest extinction event of all time. The forests are disappearing, coral reefs are bleaching, and we've reached a point where polar bears are drowning and birds drop out of the sky en masse. If there ever was a time for alternative thinking, this is it.

"We need good writers," he said. (He was the "we.") "But we can't pay right now. We don't have enough funding."

"Sorry," I told him. "I don't take assignments for free."

I thought that was the end of the conversation, but a few months later—it was March or April, I think—I listened to a voice mail and discovered that this editor had a dare for me. He said he'd been reading my blog avidly, and he wondered if I could take it up a notch: Could I live off the wild plants I was writing about, maybe for a weekend or a week? Would I blog about it for Culture Change? He thought his readers would love a survival experiment, and he would even pay me for it.

"I like this idea," I told him on the phone, pacing around my apartment. "I always wanted to be a hunter-gatherer."

The iconic image of evolution, the one indelibly inked in our brains, features that familiar progression of crouching ape to upright man. Joke versions, popular on T-shirts and coffee mugs, show a silhouette of a man with a spear devolving into a potbellied figure hunched over a computer keyboard. The implied question, however tongue-in-cheek, is, "What have we become?" Are we domesticated shadows of our former selves, wolves turned to poodles?

I was born in the early eighties, part of the last generation to come of age before electronics colonized the childhood imagination. We had television, but no Internet or cell phones, and only primitive video games, like Nintendo and Atari. My family lived in the suburbs. In the summertime I used to roll down the grassy banks of the local drainage ditch and play in the overgrown weeds there, pretending it was the Amazon jungle and that I was a wild girl. In the winter I built snow caves and pretended they were igloos. I remember daydreaming in school, feeling imprisoned inside the concrete walls of the classrooms and wondering what life would have been like if I'd been born somewhere else, somewhere exotic and tribal, or maybe in the same place but at a different time. As a grown-up I thought about it too, though it felt less like an idea and more like a deep longing for something lost.

There were times in my early twenties when I would be speeding my Ford Mustang down the highway toward the Jersey Shore with the music blasting, seat leaned back and one hand on the steering wheel, feeling good, feeling relaxed, but then a sneaky sensation would spring up inside me and I'd suddenly feel that something was off. There was an acute sense of displacement. "This is the future," I'd say to myself. "What am I doing inside a steel machine?" It felt like I was playing dress-up, as if I had been mysteriously transported to a very strange time I didn't belong in. I felt like I should be wandering in a desert somewhere, maybe staring at a fire.

Modern life creates a very strange juxtaposition, when

you think about it. "Humans living today are Stone Age hunter-gatherers displaced through time to a world that differs from that for which our genetic constitution was selected . . . Although our genes have hardly changed, our culture has been transformed almost beyond recognition during the past 10,000 years, especially since the Industrial Revolution," reads a report in the *American Journal of Medicine*, 1988.

I wondered: Is it possible to experience myself as the primal hunter-gatherer I'm wired to be while living in modern civilization, in a city?

"I'll do the survival challenge," I told the editor, "the last week of May."

࿐

I awoke the fourth day in a bleary-eyed stupor. It was an exhaustion that would not recede. I tried to ignore it. I made cleavers tea for breakfast and sipped more nettle broth for lunch. It occurred to me that I might find a good supply of weeds in a neighborhood where the landlords would be less likely to invest in landscaping, so I went with another friend to a poverty-stricken part of town fifty blocks away, past Northeast 82nd Avenue, an area teeming with meth addicts. My theory panned out: overgrown sidewalk strips abounded.[7] Most of what I found, though, was

7. One study actually found species-income correlations: Conifer trees dwell in working-class neighborhoods, fruit trees are found in the inner city, and oak trees surround people with higher incomes.

wild carrot. I was glad my friend was willing to dig them for me. I was too tired.

In the afternoon I called one of Emily's friends, Henry. He lived about ten blocks away from me. I'd never met him before, but I knew that, like Emily, he taught wilderness survival skills for a local outdoors school, and I had heard that he was a particularly resourceful fellow. "I'm out of ideas," I told him. "I've looked everywhere: our neighborhood, Forest Park, Lewis and Clark, and I can't find anything to eat except wild carrot. I don't know what to do."

"How about Sauvie Island?" he suggested.

Sauvie Island is a rural region between the Columbia and Willamette Rivers. It has some farms and nature preserves within its boundaries, as well as a nude beach popular in the hot summer months.

"I'm too foggy and out of it to drive," I told him. "I feel weak."

"I'll drive," he offered.

Henry arrived in an '81 Chevy painted with blue and white swirls and a red heart around the light-utility vehicle symbol, for LUV. I recognized him from his Facebook photos, with his thick black brows and kind, smiling eyes. We didn't talk much during the half-hour drive. My attention was drawn to the scenery along a local highway. When I looked through the passenger-side window, I saw rail yards and cylindrical fuel storage structures and shipping depots. On the other side of the street, conifer trees dotted the West Hills at the very edge of the temperate rain forest known as the Tualatin Mountains, the easternmost portion of the Pacific Coast

Range. Wilderness lived on one side, and industrial civilization on the other. We drove right down the center.

We walked along the path in an open meadow for an hour, finding little other than pineapple weed and wild carrot and bull thistle, *Cirsium vulgare*. I knew that I could eat the thistle roots in the same manner that I had eaten the burdock, but I didn't want to expend the energy to dig them up, especially because the tall plant is covered in sharp thorns. Henry did me the favor of squatting down and uprooting it. Then he pulled out a knife, sliced off the spikes on the aboveground portion, and handed me the stalk, telling me to crush the stem with my teeth to send the sugary, watery sap to my hungry lips. It amounted to less than half a teaspoon of liquid, if that.[8]

"I'm so hungry I'm at the point where I'll eat grubs," I told Henry. I believe in killing only for necessity, and this seemed to fit the bill.

"Let's go look for some," he said.

We walked off the trail and into the woods lining the meadow, looking under rocks and fallen trees for bugs to eat. We didn't find any grubs, but then we stumbled upon the biggest anthill I have ever seen. The monster mound had to be a good three feet high. Why Henry happened to have a shovel with him I can't recall, but I remember he raised it to

8. I learned later that the stalk and midrib of the leaves are edible and delicious, like celery but less stringy. If only I had known then!

his thigh and swung it—thwop!—into the dark brown heap. Soil went flying and an army of startled ants came rushing out. In the disarray we saw tiny translucent ovals about the size of Tic Tacs on the ground. Henry told me these were the eggs, and he placed a leaf on the ground.

"The ants will gather their eggs under the leaf. Watch," he said. They were so small and spread out that I could only grasp one spongy little specimen at a time between my thumb and forefinger. It reminded me of a *National Geographic* article by Mary Roach that I once read, about the dietary practices of African chimpanzees. They eat termites so small that "it's like eating cake one crumb at a time."

The eggs were so tiny that I couldn't tell what they tasted like, or even if I had swallowed them. Even worse, the ants charged up my bare feet and bit my ankles in defense of their young. The energy I was spending to brush off the military was more than I was taking in. In this sort of situation, one realizes that lazy is just another word for efficient, metabolically speaking.

"What do you think about slugs?" I asked Henry.

"I've never eaten them," he said.

"I think it's time to consider it," I replied.

Sauvie Island was brimming with slimy brown slugs. Their appearance recommended them less than their slow-moving defenselessness; in light of the ant debacle, and my prolonged hunger, they seemed worth taking a chance on. After all, don't expensive restaurants serve snails, and aren't slugs just snails without shells? We carefully picked their gooey bodies off the footpath and wrapped them in large burdock leaves to take back to my apartment.

⚘

Henry put a pot of water on the stove. He said the slugs might contain toxic bacteria, so we should boil them. I felt badly about subjecting these gentle creatures to death by hot water, but Henry assured me that the heat would amount to instant fatality. We waited until the water was bubbling rapidly and then dropped them in, one by one, at which point they immediately exploded. Their skin turned white and their guts burst out in green goo. It was exactly as disgusting as it sounds.

"You go first," I told Henry.

He turned the stove off, fished out one of the snot blobs floating in the pan, and chomped down. His horrified eyes met mine in earnest.

"It's not worth it," he said.

That night I watched a video Henry had recorded of the ant egg incident and discovered that my skin had taken on a ghostly pallor. My eyes looked strangely dilated. The black of my pupils had expanded much larger than usual, so that they seemed to overtake the brown of my iris. I didn't look well, to say the least. I wrote in my journal: "I am depressed and lightheaded, discouraged."

2

Coyote Medicine

When I sat up in bed the next morning, the fifth day, a whirl of black circles flashed in my vision, and I promptly fell back onto the mattress. When I came to a few seconds later, I felt dizzy and thirsty. I could barely muster the strength to stand up and walk to the kitchen. My body was achy and limp. My legs were so weak that I had to brace myself against the wall like an old lady who lost her walker. I knew I was in bad shape to go looking for food.

It seemed that I had two choices. I could either stay put and fast until the end of the seventh day like Gandhi without a cause, or I could quit and eat something. If I quit, though, I'd have to accept defeat. I mulled it over. On the one hand I wanted to be a warrior and finish the rest of what felt like a rite of passage. I wanted to be able to look a crow in the eye and say, "I'm like you; I know how to be wild in the city." But could involuntary fasting really be considered success in a survival experiment?

"There's a thin line between badass and dumbass," my friend Will likes to say.

When you fall on the wrong side of the line, at least you can chalk it up to a learning experience. In the Native American stories told by Choctaw author David Carson in his book *Medicine Cards,* coyote is an archetype associated with folly, the trickster spirit animal who comes to prod us when we get overconfident. When you bet too big and your plans backfire, they say that's coyote medicine.

I did what anyone would do in this situation: I logged onto Facebook. One friend offered to take me out for Thai dinner that night if I quit. My mouth watered at the thought. Another told me I should hold out. It's only three days, he said, two if I didn't count this one. But what would those days be like? I wondered. I might pass out again or become delirious, and I knew that making it to the finish line unconscious would be a dubious achievement. So I reluctantly did the sensible thing. I called my editor and told him I was through. Then I ate a sugary energy bar and some Thai food and felt a hell of a lot better.

⚡

That night, Kurt Vonnegut's catchphrase from *Slaughterhouse-Five* echoed in my brain: "So it goes." I braced myself for the slew of disappointed e-mails I would find in my inbox the next morning from readers. To my surprise, I didn't get any. Instead, this is what I found:

"There are very few people who would last as long as you did. I did something similar about thirty years ago before I became an archaeologist. I maybe lasted about three days . . . it was tough," wrote a stranger named Michael Sanders.

And:

"I loved that you stopped when you felt you needed to. You let go and trusted that it was not meant to be quite like you thought," wrote someone named Vivian Grace.

Culture Change readers were gracious, but I wasn't satisfied. I needed to know why I had failed. Why hadn't I been able to live off wild food for a week in the same place where an entire culture had done it year-round less than two centuries before?

⚘

When you want to know what Portland-area hunter-gatherers ate and how densely populated their villages were, local archaeologist Cameron McPherson Smith is the guy to talk to. He sent me his research, both published and unpublished. And as I combed through it, I realized that one of the biggest obstacles I had faced during the wild food week experiment had been the plants I ate. Dandelion and plantain were not the sort of wild food native foragers were living on in the years before white people arrived. Those are edible plants that Europeans have munched on for centuries, but they're just salad greens, and salad greens are not enough on which to live. I knew I burned far more calories searching for food than I took in that week.

It is possible to rely solely on plant foods in the wild, at least temporarily. While there are no known vegan hunter-gatherer cultures today, there are many who eat more plants than meat, or who eat meat very sparingly. Hunter-gatherer diets vary all over the world based on what kind of food is abundant and easiest to get, which in turn depends on geography and climate. The !Kung in Africa rely heavily on the mongongo nut. The first people of California based much of their diet on acorns. There is no such thing as a standard human diet.

The problem I came up against was not so much my vegetarian diet as which plant foods I ate. The most calorically dense plant parts anyone can get—the plant parts on which indigenous people once sustained a massive population—are the fruit, nuts, seeds, and roots. All are available in the summer and fall, but not the spring. The spring offers mostly leaves, and leaves are not enough sustenance, especially when you're very active. Upon reflection, I realized I hadn't considered the seasons. I'd made the blunder of viewing the city the way I view the supermarket: fast food. But nature is not like the grocery store.

Another obstacle was the landscape itself. It seemed I would find a patch of roots here and then maybe a patch of tea leaves five blocks south and then pine needles maybe ten blocks from there and nettle a half-hour drive from my home. I was wandering all over the place looking around for food, trying to cobble together meals from very disjointed sources. The land wasn't like this when hunter-gatherers lived here. There wasn't any pollution to contend with, no asphalt or concrete pavement covering the ground. For the hundreds of thousands of years prior to European American settlement, the Pacific Northwest was home to five million acres of rain forest. The rain forest stretched north to British Columbia and south to California, and it was filled with thousand-year-old trees, especially Douglas-fir and Western red cedar towering as high as four hundred feet.[9] The Chinook people set controlled fires to burn back the conifers and support a sunny oak savannah, a productive prairie stretching for miles filled with wild food of all kinds. I once heard Michael Karnosh of the Confederated Tribes of Grand Ronde give a lecture at the University of Portland about native food in the days before white settlers arrived. Elders, he said, described a veritable Garden of Eden, with fields of camas like "seas of blue as far as the eye could see, like walking through an ocean" and salmon running so thick and abundant in the Columbia River that you could walk across it. Prior to the 1840s, up to sixteen million salmon came to spawn in the Columbia each year; in the twenty-first century, it's about one million.

9. By 2011, less than 10 percent of that vast rain forest remained, and logging continues. A drive to the coast—we call it "the coast" in Oregon rather than "the beach" as they say in California, or "the shore" as they say in New Jersey—takes you past shocking views of half-naked mountains with big bald patches hacked into them. They look as they sound: demented. If this continues, as it seems to be, then the entire state could eventually be barren.

Today the Columbia is one of the most carcinogenic rivers in America. It empties into the Pacific Ocean after dividing Oregon from its northern neighbor, Washington. The governments of these states issue permits allowing industrial and municipal sources to dump billions of gallons of polluted wastewater per year, including arsenic, cyanide, pharmaceuticals, mercury, and other heavy metals. If that weren't toxic enough, the federal government dumped liquid radioactive plutonium in unlined trenches along the banks, at the Hanford Reservation, a facility upstream from Portland that once manufactured material for the atomic bomb dropped on Nagasaki, Japan, at the end of World War II. Though the site is now decommissioned, it is the most contaminated nuclear weapons site in the United States, and watchdog groups say both radioactive material and chemical waste are continuing to leak into the water on a regular basis.

The Willamette River is not much better. As it flows northward into the Columbia, splitting the city into east and west, it passes along a PCB- and dioxin-filled Superfund site at Portland Harbor and, when it rains, is regularly contaminated with pesticides and automotive run-off, as well as city sewage water. Pollution has been so endemic in this river that, as far back as 1906, the state board of health warned that swimming in it caused typhoid. Recent water quality reports by Willamette Riverkeeper found *E. coli* levels at some sites nearly ten times higher than the federal Environmental Protection Agency's standards.

It's hard to say how populated the land was here before the malaria epidemic struck. Estimates range. At the high end, some archaeologists think there may have been over one million people scattered from northern California to Alaska at a given time. In the early 1800s, Chinook people lived at a density of anywhere from one to one hundred twenty people per square mile of unpolluted wilderness. Today Portland has four thousand people per square mile of sidewalk and asphalt. No wonder, then, that I had to traverse such large distances to find food. I was operating in scarcity, the same factor that spurs hunter-gatherers around the world to wander. The Mbuti of the Congo, the Hadza of the Serengeti Desert, and the Birhor of India are all nomadic foragers who shift camp whenever gathering becomes difficult within a three-mile radius of their settlement. I did my version of that—getting in the car and driving to the forest—when I exhausted the food sources within a similar distance of my apartment.

Foragers of all species have to consider their caloric expenditures in gathering food, or else they risk starvation. In that *National Geographic* article I once read about chimpanzees, primatologist Craig Stanford likened foraging behavior among our hairy cousins to shopping at the same supermarket every day. "You don't stroll down the aisles hoping to catch a glimpse of the broccoli. You know where each item is and in which months seasonal foods are likely to be in stock," he said. Even chimps know better. I should have planned. I should have mapped my neighborhood in advance. And I should have enlisted a few friends to help out. Gathering food is an energy-intensive task. You scout, you dig, you pull, you sweat, you pick leaves one at a time, and it's tedious; it burns lots of calories and can take hours to do. That I had thought of it as an individual challenge probably reflects the influence of American culture on my mind-set more than anything else. Wilderness survival lore is invariably about one person overcoming the odds—a triumph of the ego, each person alone and out for herself—but there's no mandate that it has to be that way. For people living in real hunter-gatherer societies, it isn't like that on a day-to-day basis. People are social creatures for a reason.

A more effective strategy for an urban foraging survival experiment, I realized, would be to gather a group of friends with whom to forage and to become intimately familiar with the locations and seasonal changes of plants in my neighborhood in advance. When I thought of how urban wild animals get by, I realized that the squirrels have a brilliant idea: store nuts and fruits, the most caloric plant parts, in advance. If I was diligent in the summer and fall, I could have them on hand year-round when I needed them. This is squirrel wisdom, if you will.

"I'll do it over again," I told my editor. "I'll do it differently and I'll get it right next time."

3
Cathlapotle

Cameron McPherson Smith may be an archaeologist at Portland State University, but I prefer to think of him as the local version of Indiana Jones. He wears the two-day stubble, the adventurous spirit, and even—sometimes—a jungle hat reminiscent of the crucial fedora. Cameron digs for lost artifacts at Ridgefield Wildlife Refuge in nearby Washington State, where he has contributed important research on the remains of Cathlapotle, an ancient Chinook village. When he is not working, Cameron goes on expeditions to exotic places with harsh climates, such as the North Pole, the tropics, and the deep sea off the coast of Alaska. Last time I talked to him, he was preparing to float around in the stratosphere in a homemade pressure suit.

When Cameron offered to take me to see Cathlapotle firsthand one summer afternoon, I was thrilled. When he said he was bringing machetes so we could beat back the thorny bushes that grow there, I was even more enthusiastic because I had never gotten to wield one before, and now I could pretend I was going on a real wilderness adventure.

Cathlapotle was one of nineteen villages that the American explorers Meriwether Lewis and William Clark encountered when President Thomas Jefferson sent them west and they reached the region then known as Wapato Valley, which encompassed modern-day Portland and the nearby city of Vancouver, Washington. The Chinook people they met lived as hunter-gatherers with no domesticated animals except for dogs, which they named and treated as pets and employed as hunting companions. They also made clothing out of the dog hair, which they mixed with wool from wild goats. But that's not quite how Lewis and Clark viewed their canines, unfortunately.

On March 29, 1806, Clark wrote in his journal:

"Several tribes of the Hul-lu-et-tell Nation reside on this river. At 3 oClock P. M. we arrived at the Quath lah pah tle Village of 14 Houses on main Shore to the N.E. Side of a large island. Those people in their habits differ but little from those of the Clatsops and others below. Here we exchanged our deer Skins killed yesterday for dogs, and purchased others to the Number of 12 for provisions for the party, as the deer flesh is too poore for the Men to Subsist on and work as hard as necessary."

"Does that mean what I think it means?" I asked Cameron.

"They bought them to eat them," he said.

I wondered if the Chinook people knew what fate their beloved dogs were about to suffer. I hope so, but then, I also hope not. Those white people were savages.

As we drove there, roughly twenty-five miles north of the city, Cameron lamented that he had forgotten to bring insect repellent. "Maybe we should stop and pick some up," he said.

"The season hasn't been bad for mosquitoes," I replied. "Besides, we have long sleeves and long pants." I couldn't wait to get there.

We parked in a gravel lot and walked across a railroad bridge to a model plank house, a full-scale replica of a Chinookan ceremonial lodge. It is very large, about the length of a football field, is made of cedar wood, and is decorated with deer and bobcat hides. From the outside, it looks like a giant birdhouse. The entryway has a big cutout circle for a door. It is about four feet tall, which meant we had to bow as we walked through, as if submitting to the house. Cameron said this was an intentional design feature that made the houses more difficult to attack and gave residents time to escape via secret underground tunnels in the event of warfare. The center of the building had a long trench-shaped fireplace for cooking and heating. Chinook families used to sleep in bunks along plank house walls.

"Euro-American explorers commented on the well-being of the Indians, and from this we often imagine a sort of Garden of Eden, where food was there for the taking. But as with all myths, the real world isn't so simple," Cameron said. "If you weren't prepared, you could fail."

In 1992 archaeologists dug up the remains of fourteen buildings, each of which is believed to have housed a clan of up to one hundred people. The archaeologists wondered how so many people were able to find enough food to stay in that one place year-round. Even in the mild climate of the Willamette Valley, animals migrate during winter, salmon run in the rivers for two weeks per year, and nuts and berries—the most caloric plant foods—can only be collected in the summer and fall.

How did they do it? The answer was hiding. In a report Cameron coauthored, he wrote that researchers were surprised to discover that the floorboards of the buildings were concealing enormous cellars filled with watertight barrels, each holding fifty-five gallons worth of dried food. They estimated that each nuclear family—defined as a married couple, two children, a dog, and a few elders—probably was allotted five per year. It was like Costco down there: imagine bulk containers of acorn flour, sun-dried blackberries, and salmon jerky, just for starters. Unlike my survival foraging experiment, their version of eating wild came with food security.

The land outside the plank house is a white oak savanna ringed by a riparian forest of cottonwoods in the distance. If I were to transport myself two hundred years into the past, that is the natural landscape I would see in the urban Portland area. It's very different from the fern-draped Columbia Gorge, a collection of waterfalls east of the city that tourists tend to think is representative of the Pacific Northwest wilderness.

We walked about two miles from the model plank house to reach the site of the ancient village of Cathlapotle. It's off-limits to the general public. The hike took us on a winding footpath through wetlands with shallow pools of wapato, an aquatic edible tuber, growing in dense clusters. These were a staple food once. We heard frogs croaking and saw the arrow-shaped leaves twitch as they hopped from plant to plant, leaving tiny splashes in their wake. The trail opened into a broad, flat prairie with grass so dry and brown it looked like you could torch the place with a single match, especially with the help of the white seed-filled fluff that blows from cottonwood trees—which can, in fact, be used as a source of tinder for fire-starting.

The soil is rocky and gray and crumbly from the silt deposited by the oddly named Lake River, an offshoot of the Columbia River, which is invisible from the prairie but runs beside it. No matter where I stood, I found the air thick and humid, nothing like the city.

The grass flattened under our weight and made a rustling sound as we tromped through. We noticed the field was peppered with Eurasian weeds, especially bull thistle, plantain, and ripe Himalayan blackberries, which we picked and ate along the way.

Cameron swung his arms as we walked and cut his finger on a sharp blade of tall grass. I wished I had some yarrow, *Achillea millefolium,* a wild plant whose leaves and flowers can be applied topically to stop bleeding and pain.[10] We didn't see any that day, so I MacGyvered a makeshift

10. Yarrow's Latin name refers to the mythical warrior Achilles; it was an important plant for Roman soldiers, who used to take it into combat and apply it to their deep battlefield gashes. The second word, *millefolium,* means thousand-leaved, referring to the appearance of its feathery, finely dissected leaves. Yarrow has other neat uses too: you can rub it on your skin as an insect repellant, or dry it and drink it as a tea to combat a cold.

bandage out of a plantain leaf. I knew plantain draws out splinters and insect stingers when topically applied as a poultice—which entails chopping it up and mixing it with water to make a paste, or chewing it up and mixing it with spit, in a bind. Once I met a guy who even told me he used plantain to dull the pain of jellyfish stings. A grass cut was not a sting, and plantain is not a disinfectant herb, but the smooth, broad leaf made a decent bandage, which seemed better than nothing. I adhered it to Cameron's finger by tying it with a long skinny flower stem, and the pressure helped staunch the bleeding.

Cameron kept turning around to look behind us as we walked, saying he felt like someone was watching. We didn't see anyone, but we did come across animal scat, possibly from a coyote. When we came to a wall of thorny blackberry brambles and stinging nettle, Cameron pulled a cylindrical sling off his shoulder. Out came the machetes: It was jungle-explorer time.

"If we can get past this, we're in good shape," he said, gesturing to a faint trail beyond it.

He raised a machete above his head and swung it diagonally in front of his body to strike at the armed shrubbery. It made a delightful clanging sound as it hit the plants. "You want to let the weight of the blade do the work," Cameron said. "Be careful not to strike toward yourself because you can end up with the blade stuck in your leg, or something like that."

If I accidentally amputated a limb and bled to death in a field where cell phone signals don't work—and with yarrow nowhere in sight—my poor friend would watch helplessly and be scarred forever. What important sentiment should I speak on my deathbed? It must be something epic, profound, memorable. As I watched Cameron hack away at the brush, his back drenched in sweat, I realized I couldn't think of anything good enough. "Cameron," I said, "I'm afraid my last words are going to be, 'I have writer's block.'"

"Be careful," he said. "Branches fall without warning."

I followed him over a barbed-wire fence and onto a path of hardened mud. I kept my eyes on the ground to avoid tripping and saw a deer track followed by a feline print much larger than a dog's paw. It appeared we were in cougar territory. "Looks like that to me," Cameron agreed.

We could hear the river as we approached the dig site. I had noticed a few mosquitoes here and there on the way to the machete spot, but as we got closer to the water, they concentrated themselves into clouds that swallowed us in an awful frenzy. It was like being in a fog of suck. I slapped my arms and back ferociously and even killed three or four at a time, but it made no difference. They kept coming. "Oh my god!" I cried. "They're swarming me!"

They bit right through my cotton clothes. I was dressed in all black with a bandanna covering the lower part of my face and neck. In retrospect, I don't know why I thought the uniform for protesting the World Trade Organization at the Battle of Seattle would be the right choice for this excursion. Cameron seemed less bothered. He had on a sky blue button-down made of synthetic material.

"Have you ever been to the Amazon?" I asked him.

"Yes," he said.

"Is it like this?"

"Yes, actually," he said.

The buggers were relentless. I tried to ignore them as Cameron pointed out an extremely faint depression in the soil. He said it had been created by a plank house that had long since rotted away.

"We couldn't see it when we first came out here," Cameron said. "We went with Lewis and Clark's journal and they said it was in this area. So they described it a little bit and that gave us the idea that it was in this stand of trees. We took machetes and cut long straight lines in this vegetation. Basically we made a map. When we put the map onto the computer, then we could see the depressions. The computer made them show up. Then we came back and started putting holes into the ground where we saw depressions, and in every one of those we found artifacts."

"You dug this spot up? I can't tell."

"One of our trenches went from those trees over there to these here, like a checkerboard. This was all bare ground when we excavated."

"Did you find anything?"

"One hundred thousand objects, everything from pieces of bone from animals they were eating to all kinds of stone tools, bone-perforating tools, arrowheads," he said.

"Do you ever find mega-fauna bones?"

It was not as silly a question as it might sound. Researchers have found evidence that all kinds of giant creatures roamed the area, from elephants to sloths. In the 1960s, a fourteen-thousand-year-old mastodon skeleton was unearthed in Tualatin, a Portland suburb. Excavations for Oregon's Woodburn High School once turned up the remains of a teratorn, an extinct 170-pound bird.

"The timing isn't quite right for [mega-fauna]," Cameron said, dashing my hopes. "They died out ten thousand years ago. This village was probably abandoned in the 1830s. The house structure stood for a while, but then these cotton-wood trees grew up around the remains."

"It's not a very thick forest we're standing in," I said. We could easily see the sky.

Cottonwoods have a lifespan of only about one hundred or so years, so these were not around when the village of Cathlapotle was in existence. Few of the plants around us likely were. It's possible that an ancestor of the native orange-flowering herb beside us, jewelweed, *Impatiens capensis,* was. That one is a hiker's best friend because its leaves and stems can be split and rubbed on skin exposed to poison ivy or poison oak to prevent a rash.

"There was a big epidemic in 1833, and then it was abandoned and people left. The walls rotted and fell apart in place," he said.

The epidemic he was talking about was malaria. The disease destroyed 98 percent of the native population here. Ninety-eight. As I slapped at the relentless mosquitoes, it was very easy to imagine how that could happen. I wondered if maybe some of the bugs biting me were descended from those bugs that killed them.

The site was sprinkled with molehills, and Cameron encouraged me to look closely at them. Rodents are little excavators, often digging several feet into the soil and bringing up objects. I ran my hand over one such pile and found a chunk of charcoal, then a tiny bone fragment.

"You see how white it is?" Cameron said. "When you cook an animal and the bone is in the fire, it turns really white like that. That could easily be from the village here."

The Chinookans who lived here spoke a language called Multnomah.

"[This site] is very exciting because of the uniqueness of these foragers," Cameron said. "It represents foragers who were very different from other foragers worldwide."

"'Keep Portland weird' is an ancient concept?" I asked.

"There you go," he said.

Most hunter-gatherers live in communities characterized by egalitarianism and sharing. On the Northwest Coast, on the other hand, a quarter of the population was slaves. So it was not really the good kind of "weird."

There is evidence that people were living in the Willamette Valley, the site of modern-day Portland, since 200 AD, but archaeologists have found artifacts farther inland along the Columbia River dating to 8000 BC, and they have found structural remains of villages in central Oregon dating back to 9500 BC. Archaeologist Kenneth Ames, Cameron's colleague at Portland State University and an expert on this region, has said that he suspects that even older sites may have existed in the region, and that they are probably far underground, wedged there by ancient earthquakes.

The prevailing theory in academia is that humans originally came here from Asia by walking across a frozen

Cathlapotle

Bering Strait during the last Ice Age, where they would have encountered mammoths and lions. It is not clear how they got from there down to Oregon and beyond; some scientists suspect they sailed along the Pacific Coast, and others think they walked through an ice-free corridor.

The people who lived here changed culturally and technologically over the next eleven thousand years, shifting their dwellings from round pit houses dug in the ground to giant rectangular plank houses made of red cedar wood by around 1450 BC. The pit houses were about 15 feet in diameter, but the plank houses were majestic, commonly 460 feet long and 50 feet wide; as many as three hundred people could live inside one at a time. Each house had territorial rights to harvest certain high-value food resources, such as salmon. Two or three such houses made a village. There was frequent warfare, with different tribes raiding each other to get access to prime salmon runs. But wars, like barroom brawls, were also reportedly fought over issues of pride and infidelity. The most nefarious reason for waging war, though, was slavery. Slaves were made to do the hard work of hunting and gathering, animal processing, and cooking, while the rest of the population was free to be doing more desirable activities—fishing, woodworking, that sort of thing.

Up to 25 percent of the historic native population along the Pacific Northwest coast was enslaved, and raids between tribes were the source of the free labor. It was mainly northern tribes raiding southern tribes; the Chinook, who lived in modern-day Portland, were in between and acted as middlemen in the sale of people. It was a brutal business. Archaeologists have found bodies of middle-age slave women who were bound and decapitated. Instead of being buried, slaves were thrown out like trash when they died, sometimes into the ocean. Keeping this in mind relieves me of idyllic fantasies of what those old days might have been like.

The ancient history of the Pacific Northwest Coast also has some beautiful aspects. Native woodcarving art was famous throughout the world for its beauty and craftsmanship. The Chinese sailed across the Pacific Ocean to buy totem poles for perhaps as long as seventeen hundred years. Their influence may have been the reason for depictions of dragons seen in native art here.

The potlatch tradition, in which one household or village would fete another and prepare a year's worth of gifts to bestow upon their guests, is equally famous and has become a symbol of generosity. It also reflects the region's storied abundance of food and resources, due to the tribes' highly sustainable land management practices. They did an excellent job of respecting nature. There was no nuclear waste in the rivers, no smog in the air.

๛

Cameron gestured to the length of the depression. "Down through here you would have a ranking spectrum. The lowest-ranked people were there—"

"That's the ghetto," I offered.

"Exactly," Cameron said.

"Same kind of thing today," I said.

If you lived back then, you would be able to tell the upper-class Chinookans by their body modifications. Everyone would have a flattened forehead, because parents tied wooden boards to the front of a baby's forehead to apply pressure and mold their faces into a look considered attractive. But if you saw someone with a labret piercing—that's the one between the chin and the lower lip—then that meant that person was high status. Artists were especially respected.

"The artisans were under perpetual contract by the elite families, because they used those objects to look so great, to display their wealth. Elaborate clothing, jewelry, decoration of any kind. So the guys down here have canoes and paddles, but the guys up here have canoes and paddles that are intricately carved and painted. It's conspicuous consumption," Cameron said.

"What was the position of women like?" I asked, injecting myself into the historical village.

"It could be very high. Farther north they very often had women chiefs of the entire village. Here it was much more male-dominated; however, there were powerful women here. A lot of common women here were engaged in long-distance trade."

"They were businesspeople?"

"Yes," Cameron said. "I do know that the European collectors arrived in the mid-1800s and wanted to buy artifacts that represented a culture that, as far as they were concerned, was about to go extinct."

"They were right about that," I said.

"When the Hudson Bay Company came here initially, they didn't want the land and they didn't fight with the Indians," Cameron said. "They wanted furs to make top hats. So what they did was contract out work to native people. So actually native people had somebody they could sell stuff to who wasn't trying to take their land. But that was the 1820s. By the 1840s, the Europeans who were arriving wanted to settle here, and that's when they were driven off their land. There wasn't much fighting because [of the epidemic]," Cameron said.

By now the sun was descending and we had to hurry back to the car before the park officials locked the gate for the evening. We heard birds chattering, but they were drowned out by the wind, whooshing softly as it rolled through the cottonwood and white oak trees lining the grassland. "That sound reminds me of the ocean," I said.

"I don't like it," Cameron said.

"Why?"

"It reminds me of eternity."

"Is that a bad thing?" I asked.

"It's like watching sand in an hourglass, or listening to a ticking clock. I feel this urgency. Our precious consciousness is here for such a short time," he said.

"We're lucky," I said.

At home I counted my mosquito bites. I stopped when I got to seventy.

Okay, maybe not so lucky.

Cathlapotle

4

Squirrel Wisdom

A burst of motion caught my attention at the very edge of my peripheral vision. Above me, on a thick black telephone wire strung across an intersection, I saw a gray squirrel bound along the tightrope with something green in his mouth. I squinted and looked closer and saw that he had himself a walnut attached to a twig. It was not a ripe one, since it was only late August now, but it would be ripe soon enough. The streets were already bursting with food. Apples and plums rained down any time a breeze swept through and rustled the branches, showering the sidewalk with fruit, sun-warmed and juicy. The figs were not yet ready to eat, nor were the nuts of various kinds, but I could see them now on the branches and I knew the harvest season was coming. The summer heat would slowly fade and the nights would grow colder. In October, the trees would turn colors, their red and gold leaves like embers in a fire rising up to touch the smoke-colored sky. The wind would sweep them off their branches and splash them like paint on the cars, the sidewalk, and the road, until the whole city looked like a Jackson Pollock painting. That's when the leaves would make a crunching sound as I stepped on them, looking for chestnuts.

It was afternoon when a friend and I crouched between parked cars, gathering chestnuts by the handful. We were on a residential street lined with Victorian houses and trees so big their branches formed an archway. This was a boon: For an urban animal of any species, nuts are a particularly fortuitous find. Not only are they packed with calories, but they come encased, protected from the dirty city streets by hulls and shells.[11] In their fresh-from-the-tree form, the chestnuts look like Koosh balls, those shaggy rubber-band toys that people used to bat around with spandex rackets, because they grow inside prickly green husks. We could tell the edible chestnuts, *Castanea* spp., apart from toxic horse chestnuts, *Aesculus hippocastanum*, because the husks on the horse chestnuts have thicker, wider-spaced spikes that resemble a medieval mace.[12] The ones covering the edible chestnuts are thin and sharp, so I couldn't pick them up and open them by hand. What I had to do instead, my friend showed me, is

11. Of all the plant material you can forage in a city, flowers, fruits, and nuts are the safest in terms of exposure to contaminants, because plants don't usually bring toxins into their reproductive parts.

12. Horse chestnuts are not considered edible because they contain large amounts of saponins, which are soaplike compounds, and so eating them would, like eating soap, cause an upset stomach. But if you leach them first, they could be made edible. And you could also make use of them as soap. Author Thomas Elpel says you can slice them up and use them as laundry detergent.

pin them with my shoe—firmly, but without crushing them—and then drag my foot across the ground until a chestnut popped out. It's fun, and you have the added benefit of looking ridiculous to passersby, rather like a barnyard animal stomping around. If you have good balance and a partner to hold your hand, and if you can keep an even pressure on the chestnuts, you can take a more graceful approach and spin around like a ballerina when you do it.

I was glad to be gathering food in advance of my next wild food week; I didn't want to fast like last time. Round Two would happen at the end of November, around Thanksgiving, at the very end of the autumn season. Until then, my goal was to forage with friends and store up as many resources as I could.

Above us, squirrels flitted in the branches.

"Do you think they know we're competing for the same food? Do you think they're mad at us?" I asked my friend.

Just then, three fat chestnuts fell through the foliage and landed at our feet. When I looked up, there was a squirrel peering down at us.

"There you go, now leave," my friend said, speaking for the squirrel.

⅋

Chestnuts are easy to process: All you do is remove the husk and roast or boil the nuts. Acorns are an entirely different story. The acorn, of course, is the fruit of the oak tree. I could have called it a nut, but as far as botany is concerned, all nuts are fruits, and all fruits are fruits. It's like my dad says about my mom: "All my stuff is her stuff, and all her stuff is her stuff." There are four hundred fifty species of oak trees in the world, eighty in North America alone. Acorns have a tendency to look like Frenchmen in berets, but their appearance varies between species. Some are as round as marbles, while others are shaped like Coneheads.

"Despite their long history as a food source for people over much of the world, acorns are widely believed to be poisonous or inedible. . . . Acorns deserve better than this," writes Sam Thayer, author of *Nature's Garden*, one of my favorite foraging guidebooks.

The species native to the Portland area is called the Oregon white oak, or the Garry oak, *Quercus garryana*. It can live to be five hundred years old. Conservatively estimating that people reproduce once every thirty years, sixteen generations of the same family could eat from the same tree. Yields vary from year to year, from no acorns at all to as many as twenty-nine thousand nuts—enough to feed a whole lot of people, and squirrels, too.

Oak trees are everywhere in Portland. Their sheer abundance made them a prime candidate for my wild food cache, so I thought it auspicious when my friend Jason invited me to collect acorns with his students, a dozen young adults in a wilderness skills course he was teaching. We went to a neighborhood park—the sort with a baseball diamond and a playground—and gathered acorns by the handful, dropping them into five-gallon plastic buckets. I dared one of the students, a rugged Alaskan, to eat one raw. He crushed and peeled the shell and popped a nut into his mouth. Then his face puckered up like a raisin and his smile turned to a grimace. The bitter astringents grasping hold of his tongue, known as tannins, are not just deterrents—they have useful applications.[13] They serve to protect the trees from bacterial infection, and some people use them in hide tanning as well. If you want to eat acorns, though, you have to get rid of the tannins first. It's a process.

There is a rumor that some species have acorns that are palatable raw, but their existence is disputed and even controversial. They live somewhere between the tooth fairy and honest politicians. It is true that the concentration of bitter tannins varies widely among the different oaks, with some containing less than 1 percent and others more than 30 percent. "The 'sweet acorn,' the acorn that doesn't need to be leached, is the Holy Grail of wild foods," writes Thayer, the field guide author. "Such acorns may be native to Israel or Portugal, but not here. Dream of these tannin-free acorns if you wish, hope if you like, but don't waste your time looking for them. No acorn myth has bred more disillusionment."

At the wilderness school headquarters, we sat in a circle on the floor and took turns passing around hammers with which to crack the acorn shells. Whoever wasn't cracking the shells was peeling them to reveal the nutmeat inside. Once free of their coverings, we crushed the acorns in a hand-cranked meat grinder, then put them in a giant vat and

13. A wash made from the bark of oak trees can be used as a topical antiseptic for first- and second-degree burns.

poured big pots of boiling water over it several times to rinse out the tannins. This is just one of many ways to leach acorns. The old-fashioned method is to put the nutmeat in a porous bag and hang it from a sturdy tree branch over a rushing river for several days, so that cold water is constantly rinsing them. The modern, urban version is similar, but not for the squeamish: You can suspend a mesh bag in a toilet tank. That's the tank, not the bowl—the place where the clean cold water comes from the pipes on its way to being flushed.

After boiling, we left the nutmeat to dry off. Hours later, we pulverized it in a powerful food processor to turn it into flour. Even with a dozen people working, it took more than a day to process the nuts into flour. In light of that, it's easy to see why people evolved to be such social creatures.

⚘

My friend Jason lives in an urban homestead. He gets his electricity from solar panels, keeps chickens in his backyard, and grows much of his own food in a large garden. When I stop by his house, I usually find him working on some kind of do-it-yourself project, like brewing his own beer or sewing leather shoes by hand. He's in his late thirties, and he's a fun person to hang out with, particularly if you want to learn self-sufficiency skills. He once sent me a text message that said something like this: "Road kill deer . . . my place. Wanna help?"

Even though I had no plans to eat meat, I said yes, because animal-processing know-how might come in handy some day. Maybe I would want to get a hide or make bone jewelry. In any case I saw no moral conflict; scavenging seems better than leaving an animal to decompose on the side of the road. It's a way of being resourceful and getting local food, and it could be a respectful interaction. I wasn't sure what I was about to get myself into, but I went to it with an open mind.

༚

Though he doesn't look like it now, Jason grew up a "redneck" kid on the eastern shore of Maryland. "I got my hunting license when I was seven. I used to kill all kinds of animals: deer and squirrels and ducks and geese and whatnot. I would gut and skin and process them all," he told me.

His back porch was about to be covered in blood. A large doe with a shiny red-brown coat lay on her side. She looked to be in pristine condition except for a smashed leg, and her coloring reminded me just a little of the German Shepherd dog I grew up with. I felt fondness for her, and sadness, too.

Jason had brought one of his students there to assist him, and I stood back while she spread the animal's legs so that he could drag a knife along its underside, unzipping it like a parka from its pelvis to its neck. With sticky, bright red hands, he took a small axe and knocked it against the deer's rib cage several times until it split apart. The body cavity was filled with burgundy liquid, a result of trauma that had caused internal bleeding.

"This is illegal, right?" I said.

"Right," Jason said. "You're not allowed to have roadkill."[14]

Jason scooped out the lungs and heart with his bare hands. He set the organs in a pile next to the body. Then he took a garden hose and rinsed the blood off his deck. It streamed into the garden.

"Do you know anyone who was actually arrested?" I asked.

"Me. Federal agents came to my house," he said. He knew I was going to write about this, so he declined to tell me the details.

It was hard not to cringe as I watched him work. I had to remind myself that the doe couldn't feel pain in death. I had seen dead things before—in New Jersey, especially, the

---

14. Later, I called the Oregon Department of Fish and Wildlife and asked for the specifics on the roadkill law. Spokesman David Lane told me that in Oregon, it is illegal to pick up animals that are regularly hunted and regulated, including deer, elk, waterfowl, duck, pheasant, and quail. It is legal, though, to pick up non-protected species such as coyote and badger, and it's also legal to pick up regulated fur-bearing species such as beaver, fox, otter, raccoon or bobcat during fur-bearer season if you have licenses to do so.

Some people mistakenly think it's illegal to touch any kind of roadkill for any reason, but Lane assured me, "It is not illegal to touch an animal, it's illegal to take them into possession." So if you see a dead deer in the road blocking traffic, you won't get in trouble for hauling it out of the way. "You can definitely do that," he said. Laws applying to birds are much stricter. Under the US Migratory Bird Treaty Act, federal law bans the possession, transport, sale, or barter of migratory birds as well as their parts, eggs, and nests. This applies to native birds, including hawks and eagles and owls, even though they are often killed by cars. Even just having the intent to sell or barter a migratory bird is a felony.

Squirrel Wisdom

highways are constantly littered with road kill—but this was different—it was right there, right in front of me, and there was no looking away as I sped past.

"So the fact that you did get in trouble, is it going to stop you?" I asked.

"I'm not doing anything dreadfully wrong. I'm not harming anyone or doing anything that's going to lead to anyone getting harmed. When I pick up an animal to bring it home and butcher it, I'm doing it to eat," he said.

I was just standing off to the side, watching, until Jason asked me help him lift the doe so he could hang it from a rafter. I hesitated. This was gruesome, gruesome stuff. At the same time, I understood my participation to be a way of honoring the animal, in the way that holding a funeral honors a person, so I obliged. I squatted down, wrapped my arms around the doe's heavy body, pressed my chest against its back, and stood up, lifting with my legs. My hands were sticky with its blood.

Jason climbed to the top of a stepladder, leaned over, and slipped a rope over its neck like a noose. My stomach felt queasy.

"I feel horrible that in the fast-paced way we live—the freeways, you know—animals are victims at times, and they're so disregarded, so disrespected. People drive over them. It turns my stomach. It hurts my heart to see that. It makes me cry," Jason said.

He slid his knife into the deer's shoulder, cutting the hide from the flesh and peeling it back like a banana. He paused and looked at me.

"So yes, I know it's illegal, but my heart tells me to stop and pull over and drag this animal off the road so it won't keep getting smashed. If it was a human being, we would do that, and there's no difference between animals and human beings, really," he said.

"I agree," I replied.

"When I see roadkill, I think, 'My god, why don't I take this home and eat it?' Because there's nothing wrong with it. It made that sacrifice. It sacrificed its life unwillingly, yes, but why not use it? Why not eat it?" he said.

A few days later, he handed me a jar of deer fat as a contribution for my wild food week. It looked like mayonnaise, which was a lot easier to stomach than the sight of that doe.

⁊

Another day that fall I went to Jason's house and he took me to gather hawthorn berries. There was a tree just around the corner from where he lives in a sidewalk strip. It's interesting how the line between public and private property begins to blur when you forage in a city. If it's hanging over a sidewalk, I call it food for the taking, especially if it's growing on the side closer to the road than to somebody's house. The hawthorn, *Crataegus* sp., had formidable thorns jutting out amidst clusters of shiny red berries that reminded me of little tiny apples.[15] There are at least two hundred kinds of hawthorn species in the world, and all are edible. You can eat

15. Hawthorn, rose, and apple are all related. They're in the rose family.

the leaves as well as the berries. The berries are full of anti-oxidants; extracts made from them are popular in Europe and China for strengthening the heart, lowering blood pressure, and steadying arrhythmias. We reached up and pulled handfuls of fruit from the tree. I tasted a berry and found the flesh to be bland, and there were lots of seeds in the center, but I wasn't going to be picky. I wanted to have as much food as I could gather. I read later that one traditional way of preparing hawthorn on the Northwest Coast is to bake it into fruit leathers, so I decided to pop them in my fridge and try making them in my oven during the wild food week.

When you hang around Jason long enough, you're bound to hear some stories you wouldn't have heard otherwise. He reads a lot of obscure things, especially about his ancestors, the nomadic hunter-gatherers whose descendents became German and Irish people.

"Their societies were set up in a very similar way to the way Native American societies were set up before agriculture," he told me. "There are some great stories about when they met the Romans, who were agriculturalists. The Romans came in with their disciplined legions and started fighting with them. And in order to fight the Romans, the Germanic tribes developed a standing army, like the Native Americans—Crazy Horse tried to do that. In order to feed their standing army, they had to start growing grains, rye, and things like that to make bread, and it really freaked the Germanic folks out, because being hunter-gatherer herder folks, it was against their nature to compel the Earth to feed them, to dig it up and to plant things and to wait for it. And also, to seed felt like bad luck to them, because they were used to taking what was available, not compelling Earth to give."

"That makes sense. I get that, as a forager," I said.

"What really freaked them out, too, were the large fields of grain moving in the wind. It was really eerie to them. They would say 'The wolf is in the wheat,' or 'The wolf is running through the rye.' And when they harvested the rye—these superstitions and traditions built up over time—they would yell and scream as they were scything the grain down because they imagined they were chasing this bad-luck animal spirit through the grain. They would get down to the last bundle and they would grab it and bind it, like, bind that bad luck."

"Agriculture is bad juju?" I asked.

"Yeah, because you're compelling the Earth to give you something that is not already provided," Jason said. "They learned from the Romans to build grinding wheels using river power to drive the stones, and that really scared them, too. In compelling the rivers to work for them, they felt like they were enslaving nature, and that felt really bad to them. That's why there are so many stories throughout Medieval Europe where the miller is a supernatural character and the grain mills are always located outside the city limits, because it felt unnatural to folks to be using the river to drive the mill. It was so contradictory to the way they had lived."

॰॰

After we gathered the hawthorn berries, Jason took me to some overgrown alleyways where we found a stand of yellow dock, *Rumex crispus*, a common weed with long, smooth, arrow-shaped leaves flecked with purple splotches. Its leaves are edible raw or boiled,[16] and its telltale rust-colored seed stalks grow three feet tall and close behind. The leaves are high in vitamin C and zinc, and the seeds can be quietly smuggled into baked crackers or even your morning oatmeal. Harvesting them is simple, Jason showed me. I grasped a stem and slid my hand from bottom to top, brushing the seeds right into a paper bag. I didn't have a shovel with me at the time, but if I had, I could have dug up the roots, boiled them, and drank them as a detoxifying tea. Online, merchants advertise yellow dock root extracts as iron supplements as well as for chelation, or removing heavy metals from the body.

"Jason, do you ever wish you lived back in the days of your ancestors?" I asked.

"No, it's not like I wish I lived a thousand years ago," he said.

"You don't?"

"No," he said. "We live in this golden age with electricity and motor cars. I can play in bands and tour and go to cities. I can get in a plane and time travel to the East Coast in six hours—a path that would have taken months under the power of my own walking. But you know, this can't last forever—cars and trucks and grocery stores and power plants

16. Like spinach and rhubarb, yellow dock contains oxalic acid, which can bind with calcium, preventing absorption. Most people have no trouble, but it can be an issue if it is consumed in large quantities or for anyone with kidney disease.

and all that kind of stuff. We've really forgotten a lot in this industrial age that we live in. I think part of what I'm doing here is to help remember a few things to inspire maybe a few other people—if they're lucky enough, or maybe unlucky enough—to survive what's coming."

"I would like you on my apocalypse survival team," I said.

5
Thanksgiving

The door swung open and customers streamed in to the popular restaurant to eat breakfast. I wasn't one of them. Outside on the sidewalk, I was picking mint and mallow leaves, *Malva neglecta*. It was the first day of my November wild food week challenge, and I was gathering ingredients to make a nourishing tea. I pulled pine needles in front of my apartment complex and ripe red berries from an ornamental rose bush next door. I boiled the plants together on my stove and happily enjoyed the result: The pine and rose flavors added complexity to the mint, and the mallow gave the tea a thick and creamy texture.

Like the first time I tried eating wild in the city for a week, the rules for this challenge meant everything would have to be foraged within the Portland metro area and nothing could be purchased, Dumpster dived, or gleaned from gardens. This time, though, I came into it prepared. I stocked my kitchen with jars of roasted chestnuts, acorn flour, hawthorn berries, yellow dock seeds, deer fat, and even a gift of dried stinging nettle from Jason, which I could make into tea or sprinkle into food for added nutrition.

In the afternoon, Emily came over to help me turn the chestnuts into flour and make the hawthorn berries into fruit leathers. The chestnuts were easy: We scored the shells with an "x" and put them in the oven at 300 degrees for forty-five minutes. Then we took them out, peeled the shells with our fingernails, and ate fresh-roasted nuts. I saved the rest to pulverize into flour in Henry's food processor later.

Making hawthorn fruit leathers took a little more effort. Our only ingredients were water and berries, but this was not for lack of imagination. Emily had recently tried to get wild honey after she discovered a beehive in the hollow of a tree near the Willamette River in Oaks Bottom Park.

"One night I was drinking a gin and tonic in my house by myself," she told me, "and I got this notion that I wanted to make a hot toddy with wild honey." The idea inspired her so much that she made a tipsy escapade to the woods, lighting her way with a headlamp.

"I knew which tree the bees were in because of the shape of it—there was a branch coming off in a V," she said. "I had that burlap bag that I always have, and I had on my long wool coat and wool pants, wool mittens, and a hat. I was basically planning that the bees would attack me. I left only my face uncovered. I even taped my wrists so the bees couldn't go up my coat sleeves. And for smoking them out, I had a stick of what I call beach wormwood, some kind of mysterious *Artemisia* that grows on the beach of the Willamette River."

"Did you light it?" I asked.

"Yeah," she said. "I sprayed 'em with water too—it was pretty mean. It was nighttime so the bees weren't moving around. They were just crawling and not flying. I tried to scrape the honey with a spoon but I couldn't get anything out except wax. I did take that home and used it to make little wax seals. I made little tubes out of Japanese knotweed and put a wax seal on the bottom and a cork on the top so I could have a little tube of medicine."

"Did you get stung?"

"Yeah. I got stung a couple times on my hands through the gloves. I got in my car and went home, and when I took off my coat in my bedroom, there was still a bee inside," she said.

The next time Emily tried to get honey, she brought some friends with her, including Henry. They filmed what happened next: Henry exhaled his cigarette in the bees' direction, trying to smoke them out of their hive. As you probably expect, it didn't work. He got stung.

Emily told me this story while we crushed the several cups of hawthorn berries I had gathered with Jason. I wanted to make them into a gooey paste that we could separate into strips and bake. It turned out to be more complicated than that. The paste was full of seeds that we couldn't manage to separate from the flesh. First we tried using a food mill I'd borrowed from Jason, a little metal pot with a hand-crank and a sieve, but it didn't put enough pressure on the paste, so we scooped the berries out and pressed the paste against a metal screen, rubbing it through by hand. This was tedious, messy, and mildly painful—scraping against the screen irritated our fingers. But finally we got enough to make little fruit rectangles, and I cooked them in the oven for two hours on a low setting.

While the hawthorn was baking, we stuck the dried chanterelles in a bowl of water to rehydrate them. I was looking forward to these. Mushrooms hold the peculiar distinction of being neither plant nor animal, and their hair-thin root system is mind-blowingly cool. Mycologists, mushroom scientists, have shown that these underground nets actually shuttle nutrients and even chemical messages between trees like an earthen Internet. The mycelia, as the nets are called, can be thousands of acres large, and the fruits they send up— the mushrooms—can all be part of the same organism even if separated by many miles. If it sounds out of this world, well, it just might be. Some scientists think mushrooms spores first landed on Earth by way of a meteor from outer space.

I took the jar of deer fat Jason had given me out of the fridge and unscrewed the lid. Using a spoon, I put a glob of it in a saucepan to sauté the chanterelles. They slid around in the fat and cooked until golden brown. Then we put them on a plate to let them cool. When we pierced the fungi with our forks and brought them to our lips, we were disappointed to find the flavor awfully gamey. It was, frankly, like eating rotten gym socks—so disgusting I decided I would rather be hungry than eat the rest. (Sorry, deer.) "Not again!" I thought.

The hawthorn squares turned out better, though they were mildly bitter.

On the second day, I went to get figs at Whitaker Ponds Nature Park, which used to be a junkyard. It's not the only less-than-pristine wilderness area around town: Smith and Bybee Lakes Wildlife Area, popular with Portland birders, sits on top of a landfill, as does Oaks Bottom Park. Contamination is an unfortunate fact of life in urban settings, as urban farmer types are well aware. In particular, the toxins found in urban soil tend to be heavy metals, pesticides, and the industrial chemicals known as PCBs (polychlorinated byphenols).

Tests done on urban gardens in cities across the country have detected dangerously high levels of the heavy metals lead, cadmium, and arsenic. Lead contamination is a result of the prolific use of lead paint and lead pesticides in decades past, as well as leaded gasoline, lead batteries, and lead plumbing. If ingested, lead can cause problems in mental functioning, muscle pain, nerve problems, and infertility. Arsenic was once used as a weed killer and in high concentrations can cause blindness, paralysis, and cancer. Cadmium is also carcinogenic; it's found in paint, batteries, and car exhaust, and is a by-product of coal and oil burning.

Foragers can be exposed to these contaminants by ingesting soil particles, inhaling them, or touching them. "Most people assume the danger is in eating plants that have taken up contaminants, but direct exposure to the soil seems to have the greater risk," said Jenn Bildersee, a City of Portland official who works on urban agriculture projects in contaminated areas.

To what degree this causes harm ultimately depends on the type of contaminant, the amount of the contaminant, and how long and how often exposure occurs. As common sense would suggest, sites with a history of industrial use tend to have more dangerous chemicals and higher degrees of contamination than places that have long been residential areas. Heavy metal contamination is usually highest next to buildings and in areas with lots of traffic, or where buildings with lead paint used to be.

Eating plants foraged from contaminated ground is not my first choice, but it is not always as risky as it sounds. Many contaminants do not make it into the plants because they are not available for absorption due to the composition of the soil. Plant roots growing in soil with lots of lead usually do not absorb it, for example, unless the soil is acidic or low in organic matter. Even when they do absorb it, the heavy metals tend to bind to the roots, so movement to other plant parts is limited. Studies have found lead contamination highest in roots and leaves and lowest in fruit and other reproductive parts. Washing leaves can remove up to 80 percent of lead contamination deposited via dust, and much can also be removed by peeling roots.

One study found that high-traffic areas can have ten times more lead in the soil than other places. I wanted to know how bad the situation is in Portland, so I called up Alan Yeakley, a scientist specializing in urban ecology at Portland State University. Dr. Yeakley did a study of heavy metal contamination in twenty-nine soil samples taken from the top six inches of bioswales all over the city.

Located along curbsides, bioswales are essentially fancy ditches with plants growing in them, and they're designed to capture rainwater and filter it through the soil to keep water-soluble pollutants in the runoff from getting into the storm drains and contaminating streams and rivers. Portland is not the only city to embrace bioswales, but it is among the most enthusiastic. As of 2012, it had installed thirteen hundred. Some of the older bioswales in Dr. Yeakley's study had been in commission for six years.

When he took my phone call, Dr. Yeakley was not yet ready to publish the results, but he was, fortunately, still happy to talk to me about what he and his colleagues had thus far discovered. Initially, he said, he and his fifteen collaborators hypothesized that they'd find significant contamination in the bioswales, and that the bioswales exposed to the most traffic would have the highest levels of contamination.

"We really didn't find that," he told me. "It's encouraging and surprising that a buildup of toxins really hasn't occurred. That's not to say that it won't."

I thought it sounded almost too good to be true.

"We did find slightly higher concentrations of copper, lead, and zinc, versus background soil, but nothing above the levels you'd be concerned about for human consumption, nothing that really pegs the chart. There were a few random samples out of a couple hundred that did come up a little bit higher than plant toxicity levels, but only slightly, and those were for lead and copper," Dr. Yeakley said.

"What does that mean for a forager like me?" I asked.

"It might affect plant growth somewhat but probably doesn't affect human consumption—and that's my speculation based on EPA standards," he said.

The tricky thing is that there's no consensus on what constitutes "safe." While the EPA invented limits called "Soil Screening Levels" to evaluate Superfund sites for cleanup, and states also have limits for contaminants, these are not necessarily applicable to land used for urban food cultivation or foraging. The good news is that contaminated soil doesn't have to stay contaminated. It's possible to use microbes to neutralize PAHs, PCBs, and pesticides, and all kinds of neat experiments are being done with mushrooms. And while it is very difficult to remove heavy metals from soil using natural methods, it is possible to alter their bioavailability so that they won't get into food plants.

Air pollution may be significantly more problematic for urban foragers than soil contamination, and harder to remedy. A report issued by Oregon's Department of Environmental Quality in 2012 tested a number of sites in the city and found many dangerous chemicals and heavy metals floating in the air near or above the state's standard levels for health, including benzene, polycyclic aromatic hydrocarbons, 1,3-butadiene, acetaldehyde, naphthalene, arsenic compounds, manganese compounds, cadmium compounds, paradichlorobenzene, and trichloroethylene. These largely unpronounceable substances are known to cause various kinds of cancers and diseases of the nervous system, lungs, blood, kidneys, and other organs. Some are ingredients in mundane products like mothballs and toilet cleaner; others are released as fumes from dry cleaning, cigarette smoke, and car exhaust. Higher concentrations are found in densely populated neighborhoods, near busy roads and highways, and in areas with business and industrial activity.

⚘

For lunch, I made acorn-flour pancakes. I mixed the acorn flour with water and then fried it in oil I squeezed by hand out of black walnuts.

Like chestnuts, black walnuts fall from the trees in disguise. Their hulls look like smooth green tennis balls, and like the leaves, they have a fresh, citrusy scent. They turn black and gooey as they ripen, staining everything they touch a shade of brown, including your hands. Once you wash the hulls off, you leave them to dry and then you remove the shells, which takes some effort. Their walls are too thick to break with a conventional nutcracker, so I use what I call the rock-and-block method: I put them on a concrete block and then I smash them against it with a heavy rock. The shells went flying all over the carpet and the nutmeat wasn't easy to dig out with my fingernails, but I was glad when I managed it, because they taste like English walnuts except sweeter and richer, as if they came with maple syrup and butter mixed in.

⚘

Unlike the wild food week I attempted in May, this one was going smoothly. I had stored enough food that my daily foraging excursions were fun and easy instead of stressful, and I settled into a kind of routine based around acorn pancakes and figs. The most ambitious thing I attempted was dinner on the third day. Now, ambition is a relative thing. I have a tendency to avoid recipes with more than three steps and to go through lengthy phases where I buy Mexican burritos more often than I cook. But that evening I had the grand idea to make an elaborate wild food equivalent of a Hot Pocket. I roasted chestnuts in the oven, de-shelled them, smashed them with my rock and block, and then I put the pieces in a coffee grinder to turn them into flour. Then, I mixed the flour with water to make a ball of dough, added a bit of acorn flour, stuffed in rehydrated chanterelles and stinging nettle, and baked this concoction in the oven. To my own surprise, it wasn't half bad. The only problem was the texture, because the stinging nettle leaves were dry.

On the fourth day I gathered sumac fruit, *Rhus typhina*, from a neighbor's ornamental tree. Because the scarlet, oblong fruits stay colorful even over the winter, it's popular in suburban landscaping. High in vitamin C, potassium, calcium, and antioxidants, sumac fruit is ground up and used as a spice in Middle Eastern cooking. Say the word "sumac" in America, though, and most people shudder because they think of the poison kind, *Rhus vernix*. It's easy to tell them apart, at least when they're fruiting. The edible one is a cluster of fuzzy red berries, whereas the poison kind has white berries.

༄

On the fifth day my friends and I waded neck deep into the frigid waters of Catfish Slough. With the help of a map, some rented wetsuits, and a permit from park officials, we harvested wapato. It grows underwater, so if you want to gather it in the fall you first have to visit in the summertime when you can see its distinctive arrow-shaped leaves. Because they die and fall off, leaving you very little visual marker for harvest time, you need a good memory. Fortunately, Henry was familiar with the area and led us to a patch without any trouble.

Wapato is native to North America and has been eaten by indigenous people across the continent for thousands of years. Before people, mammoths used to munch on it. Today, a cultivated variety of wapato is an ingredient in Asahi beer, a Japanese brand distributed in American stores. The plant is also used for environmental cleanup work because it absorbs heavy metals. That it was growing downriver from where the Willamette and Columbia waterways meet suggested that it was probably contaminated, but I tried not to think about it too much. Sometimes, ignorance is bliss.

Emily came with me that day, along with two other guys we knew from the local wilderness school, including the Alaskan who ate the raw acorn on a dare, and Ariel, a short, quirky little fellow who laughs with a shriek more than a giggle. Ariel is a one-of-a-kind guy; he's known to declare himself a squirrel and hop around with his elbows bent and hands limp at his shoulders. This is not as strange as it sounds. At a potluck dinner that Henry once hosted, we all sat around and thought of each other as animals. We decided that Emily is a fox because she's quiet, stealthy, and clever; that Henry is a beaver because he's always building things—cob ovens, rocket stoves, gardens; and that I was probably a raccoon, on account of being an urban forager. It also seemed fitting because I stay up late at night and wear black eyeliner. In fact, the moment I could imagine living in the woods was the moment I realized that mixing wood ashes and water makes black eye shadow.

I could feel my rubber boots filling with gooey sludge as I hopped up and down in the water. I was working to loosen the mud on the swamp floor. The Alaskan and his girlfriend paddled out to deeper water in a kayak. Emily splashed in the water beside me, also loosening roots. Tubers floated to the surface, coming up with little bubbles streaming all around them.

The wapato looked strikingly unlike any plant I had ever seen before. They are oval-shaped bulbs just a shade bigger than a robin's egg in pastel blues, pinks, and lavenders. Emily and I scooped them up and handed them to the people in the kayak, who collected them in plastic bags. When we boiled them later, they tasted just like potatoes. Historically, indigenous people cooked them in watertight, wooden boxes, heating the water with stones pulled straight from a fire.

That night I retired to my apartment feeling tired, but not hungry.

$$\mathcal{S}$$

The last day of the challenge fell on Thanksgiving, and my friends and I planned to celebrate with a wild feast at Emily's place for dinner. We would each bring foraged food from spots we knew well. Usually I spend Thanksgiving with family and think of it, like many people do, as a celebration of gratitude and generosity. But as it approached this time, it seemed more meaningful. I thought about what happened to the first people after the historic feast it commemorates, and I realized that it could be seen, in a sense, as a prelude to genocide. The fate of indigenous hunter-gatherers and agriculturists in North America after European contact became a tragic tale of biological warfare, broken treaties, and treachery. The natural landscape, too, went from sustainably managed to largely destroyed. How morbid that today our culture glosses over all that and turns Thanksgiving into a lighthearted occasion with paper turkeys in grocery store windows and talking pumpkins on TV. No one can change the past, but it is possible to observe the harvest-time feast with consciousness instead of denial. We can see it as an occasion to honor Earth's wild abundance as well as the first people and their way of life.

When I walked into the kitchen, everyone was milling about preparing dishes. Emily sat at the kitchen table cutting rose hips with a knife. She sliced the berries in half, used her fingernails to dig out the little white seeds inside, and then she put them in a saucepan with some water to boil. The next time I looked over, she had reduced the mixture into a bright orange paste. I dipped a spoon in it and found that it tasted a lot like cranberry sauce, except without the sour kick.

I mixed water, chestnut flour, and yellow dock seeds and formed the mixture into balls that would become wild scones in the oven. Ariel wrapped cattail shoots, *Typha latifolia,* in aluminum foil and baked them on the shelf below. [17]

The Alaskan manned the stove and sautéed roadkill venison with rosemary. Someone else brought stinging nettle, which we steamed, along with boiled wapato and chanterelle mushrooms. When it was time to eat, we set the food on a long, low coffee table in Emily's living room. It was an impressive display: rose hips sauce, roasted cattail, nettle, mushrooms, wapato, venison, scones, and even wild beer. Ariel was on a home-brewing kick, and he had infused this batch with yarrow and leaves from a juniper tree.[18]

17. Cattail is a common wild plant that grows in marshy spaces and roadside ditches. It looks like a reed; its top that looks like a hot dog on a stick. The entire plant is edible, from the shoots in early spring to the powdery pollen in late summer to the starchy rhizomes in the winter. Cattail is known to absorb pollutants. If you gather it from a place that's contaminated, you can still use the cattail leaves for weaving—Emily was into making mats and sun hats with them.

18. Because it is highly aromatic and slightly bitter, yarrow was widely used in place of hops in ancient Europe, and some books claim that it works synergistically with alcohol to enhance intoxication. In drinking Ariel's brew, I did notice a difference.

As I dug my fork into rose hips sauce and took a bite of a wild scone, I looked back on the week and thought myself lucky to have friends who would help me for no reason except that they wanted to. Even when I offered to return the favor by offering them some wild herbs, they dismissed the idea.

"The sun warms the Earth and never once does it say, 'You owe me,'" Ariel said, paraphrasing the Persian poet Hafiz.

PART TWO:

Mountain Medicine on a One-Way Street

6

Outlaws

The way was thick and slow with traffic as we passed modest homes in muted colors, and drab strip malls, and a Starbucks, until at last the road narrowed and the view greened. Moss-covered trunks leaned over the winding road, their branches poking through telephone wires. Emily and I drove through the hilly southwest section of the city en route to a state park, where we were going to harvest a powerful medicinal plant, Oregon grape, *Mahonia aquifolium*. It works as an herbal antibiotic and antiviral that can be used internally and externally to treat strep throat, pneumonia, staph infection, pink eye, gonorrhea, and syphilis, as well as infections caused by E. coli and Giardia.[19] The plant has shiny leaves that resemble holly. Its bright yellow blossoms are the state flower of Oregon, and it lives in conifer forests throughout western North America from Alberta, Canada,

---

19. Oregon grape has other medicinal qualities, too: It is also a liver stimulant.

down to New Mexico, and east to the Rocky Mountains. I often see it around Portland as part of the landscaping in gardens and strip malls.

Oregon grape's medicinal compounds are concentrated in its edible blue berries and in its roots. Since it was early winter, the berries were gone. The tricky thing is that digging up roots in a state park is illegal in Oregon. The regulations allow you to take berries and mushrooms, but you can't harvest anything else unless you're a scientist with a permit for study, or unless you can prove you come from Native American descent. People who just want to gather medicine for themselves or their families, but have different genes, are facing legal trouble, which means Emily and I would be outlaws on account of our parentage.

It doesn't happen often, but foragers do sometimes get busted. In New York City, foraging expert Steve Brill found himself in handcuffs for picking a dandelion in Central Park. It was 1986, and Steve was leading one of his plant identification tours, occasionally plucking a leaf here and there to show his class. He knew he was technically flouting the laws, but he didn't think much of it. After all, plants grow back, especially weedy ones. He believed his students that day were a group of college kids from Columbia University and a married couple, because that's what they told him, but it turned out that the couple was actually a pair of undercover agents on a sting operation. "They were taking pictures," Steve remembers. "I would hold up a specimen, only I was the specimen. They paid me with marked bills."

"How did they get you?" I asked him.

"One of the rangers hid behind a tree with a walkie-talkie: 'There he is on 81st Street.' Every park ranger in New York City popped out from behind the bushes. They put me in handcuffs and arrested me for eating a dandelion." It's one thing to pick plants on the east side of Portland, where neighborhoods sprawl out rather than up and vegetation abounds. The greenery here is helped along, no doubt, by climate conditions that mimic a chilled grocery-store mister. Foraging is quite another thing in New York City, with its four seasons and skyscrapers and thick, rush-rush-rushing crowds swarming the streets. I think of Manhattan as a kind of apocalypse in the present tense, a futuristic wasteland. Everything is lifeless and gray, save for the eyeball-assault of flashing signs trying to trip you into an orgy of overconsumption. As I walked around Midtown and the West Village in the fall of 2011, in town on literary business, I noticed that what little vegetation I did see was corralled. The sidewalk trees had little fences around them—gingko, mostly, but also other pollution-tolerant species, like locust. The smaller plants were carefully contained in planters. And even the city's green jewels, Central Park in Manhattan and Prospect Park in Brooklyn, are encased inside limestone walls. New York ghettoizes its greenery, keeps it caged, incarcerated, as if trees are dangerous and their escape would pose a threat to the greater metropolis.

Steve's arrest was big news in the New York media. In one *Associated Press* story, with a headline that read, "Planted Decoys Nab Foraging Botanist," Parks Commissioner Henry

Stern was quoted as defending the crackdown, saying, "Parks are to look at." [20]

This idea that we should treat parks like museums or botanical zoos is as pervasive as it is destructive. A park official in Portland once told me that his fantasy is for visitors to traverse the woods in elevated glass tunnels suspended in the trees, instead of walking on the dirt. To me that sounds about as fulfilling as staring at a postcard with the window open. Though conservationist ideals ostensibly arise from the noble desire to protect and preserve nature, they ultimately have the opposite effect, because walls keep out as much as they keep in, and it is this profound separation that has led our civilization to thrash the planet in the first place. It's hard to feel anything but vague affection or sentimental attachment for other species when we don't tangibly interact with them or perceive their utility in our day-to-day life.

The Wilderness Act of 1956 defined "wilderness" as "an area where the earth and its community of life are untrammeled by man." Barely 3 percent of the lower continental United States fits that definition today. Few politicians are committed to protecting what we have left, let alone expanding it, and those who do stump for the wilderness tend to do so on account of its beauty or out of abstract arguments for moral obligation, which are weak selling points against digging up fossil fuels or selling lumber. Though tragic, this is

20. In 1858, landscape architect Frederick Law Olmsted won a design competition to expand Central Park. His vision was to create a three-dimensional "series of naturalistic pictures."

an inevitable consequence when we forget who we are. We have lost our forests because we have forgotten what they mean to us.

We see evidence of this in popular discourse whenever anyone speaks of the land as if it is a thing, using that sterile sounding phrase "the environment." What is an "environment"? It is a setting, an ambience. The term is so abstract it could be a room in a spaceship on Mars. Similar problems arise when people talk about "vacant lots," as if a green space without a retail shop is empty, as if it is not already filled with an array of plants and animals. To a forager, land is never vacant.

The park official that blasted Steve Brill was expressing the widespread belief that touching nature is an inherently destructive practice, and that simply is not true. If it were, how could we explain our existence on this planet? Humans are integral to ecosystems. We evolved interacting with plants. When we disturb them, it can be a good thing. The federally endangered San Francisco lessingia, *Lessingia germanorum,* a tiny sunflower, requires periodic disturbance to perpetuate itself. Even in more sensitive places, foraging doesn't appear to cause forests undue stress. Portland naturalist John Kallas has taken thousands of foragers out to harvest in the same area of local parks over recent decades, and he reports little to no noticeable impact. Brill reports the same thing in New York. Perhaps this is because foragers, by and large, gather small quantities of plants for themselves and their families and almost never sell what they gather, according to statistics compiled by multiple researchers. It is in a forager's interest to have a sustainable impact if she wants to be able to return to her spot. Documented cases of overharvesting are uncommon outside of commercial motivations;[21] goldenseal and ginseng wound up on the endangered species list because profiteers saw them as merchandise with low overhead and got greedy with the scale of their gathering, not because too many people wanted to collect roots for their grandmas.

ꩠ

The Oregon grape harvest would be my very first stealth mission. If Emily worried about getting caught by park rangers, she didn't show it. Quiet as usual, she turned into the parking lot and slipped a ten-inch trowel into her burlap tote before we headed for the trail. I was grateful for the canopy of Douglas-fir and western hemlock, *Tsuga heterophylla,* because the trees blocked the cold rain from hitting our shoulders. Our lips blew vapor clouds in the frigid winter air as we hurried along the dirt-and-gravel path.

Some people have fantasy football teams. I have a fantasy apocalypse team, a crew I want in my corner if society

21. Anthropologist Rebecca McLain of the Institute for Culture and Ecology and mushroom expert David Arora each published studies on mushroom gathering in the Pacific Northwest in peer-reviewed journals, showing that foragers harvesting fruiting bodies of fungi in the popular hot spots of Sisters, Oregon, and McCloud, California, did not damage their respective ecosystems and did not diminish the mushrooms' abundance in subsequent years. However, misguided government regulation and harassment of foragers did cause harm, traumatizing children and disrupting cultural traditions. See *Further Reading.*

collapses, taking electricity and grocery stores with it. In this thought experiment I draft Emily as my scout. She is the kind of person who can slip in or out of a crowded room unnoticed, and it is precisely this trait that once supported her long and mostly successful career as a shoplifter. "American Apparel is the best place to steal from," Emily wrote on her blog, *Tracker of Plants.* "No security tags to cut out, no cameras to hide from, and as part of the code of hipness employees must swear an oath never to confront a shoplifter. So even if they stopped looking at themselves in the mirror . . . long enough to notice what you were doing and hadn't quite perfected their moral apathy enough to not care . . . you have until the police show up before you get caught." This explained her closet of stylish clothes despite her graduate school loans.

She wasn't a reckless or indiscriminate thief. Emily had a sort of Robin Hood ethos to her stealing: Only take from those who deserve it. Or as she put it, "Corporations are destroying the world anyway." I was under the impression that she was a ninja with an unblemished record until the night I saw her mug shot in *Busted,* the who's-in-jail-now newsletter that goes for $1 at the local convenience store. The photos are usually so outlandish that the paper could alternatively be titled "Meth Addicts Weekly." It was lying on her kitchen counter. When I asked about it, she admitted that she'd gotten caught stealing dresses from American Apparel. And this was how her stick-it-to-The-Man guerilla campaign ended. But not before she went back to American Apparel and stole a few more items for revenge.

The rain fell in a fine mist, the way it often does in the Portland winter, and the ground was soft and wet, so I got a bit nervous when Emily veered off the path and strode without hesitation into the sword ferns off the trail. I wasn't used to walking on anything but even ground. The city surfaces are all paved and smooth; the forest floor was full of lumps and slippery obstacles. I moved gingerly, ever conscious of the threat of twisting an ankle on the uneven surface or getting poked in the eye by an errant twig. Emily glided through the woods with no trouble at all, bobbing and weaving over mushroom-covered logs and under branches with a fast and familiar ease. Raised in rural northwestern Pennsylvania, she had grown up trekking off the path. She was so comfortable in the woods that, when she had an argument with her mother after college, she ran away to the Allegheny National Forest by herself, found a rock cave to live in, and slept there for three weeks.

I trailed her down a steep bank and across a slippery creek bed, breaking my speed for a moment to rest against the broad trunk of a Western red cedar tree. I pressed my hand against its soft bark and looked up in time to see Emily sink into the underbrush and disappear. I found her squatting over a woody shrub, about three feet tall, with shiny green leaves that resembled holly: Oregon grape.

Emily grabbed the base of the stem and yanked, pulling muddy, finger-thick rhizomes to the surface. She pulled a pair of scissors from her bag and snipped a foot-long section of the root, wiping away the wet soil to show me a bright yellow substance staining the inner bark. This was the berberine, the antibiotic.[22]

Even as we uprooted the Oregon grape, we took care to avoid killing the plant. Because Oregon grape reproduces itself both through seeds in the berries and by horizontally spreading its rhizomes, it's possible to cut off a piece of the root and replant the rest an inch or two below the dirt and come back to find new stalks later.

Emily smuggled the roots into her bag. As we hiked back toward the parking lot, I kept an eye out for passersby and park officials. It was a thrill to get away with our loot.

"I kind of feel like we're shoplifting," I said as we walked.

"Hmm," Emily replied, pondering my analogy. There was a long pause. "Yeah."

It wasn't that I felt we were stealing so much as that I related to the sense of taboo, of acting outside the law. We were doing something for which society doesn't hold a space. I felt no guilt, because my heart tells me that no one can own a community of plants and animals any more than someone can own a village of people. My loyalties are to the woods and the plants therein. I care about the sustainability of my actions out of respect for nature and as a practical matter

---

22. Berberine is also found in other plants, including coptis, *Coptis* spp., barberry, *Berberis* spp., and goldenseal, *Hydrastis canadensis*. It would be reductive to say that berberine is the sole reason Oregon grape is antibacterial and antiviral. Herbs have many, many compounds within them—some of which scientists have yet to study—and they may work together synergistically.

of wanting to be able to come back and get more medicine. These things matter much more to me than rules made by government officials.[23]

I went to purchase some vodka with which to make the medicine on the way back from the woods. At that time I was living in a run-down neighborhood along the outskirts of the city that locals refer to as Felony Flats; the nearest liquor store was on a street that doubled as a catwalk for hookers. It was the kind of area where the alcohol had to be kept behind the counter. When I asked a clerk for Everclear, he eyed me suspiciously, even taking down my license information.

"I'm making medicine with it," I explained. "With plants."

"Oh, like the Russians do," the clerk said, handing me back my ID.

At home in my kitchen I cut the Oregon grape roots into pieces lengthwise and split them in half to increase their surface area. I washed them under running water in the sink and then packed them into a glass mason jar. The only ingredients I needed to turn them into medicine were water and alcohol. I was making a tincture, a medicinal extract of the herb. The folk method for making most any kind of tincture is to fill a

23. That said, I have since discovered that officials have very little ability to enforce their regulations due to understaffing, and that some are actually sympathetic to wildcrafters, to the point where they will sometimes grant us permission or agree to look the other way when we do them the courtesy of asking. (Your mileage may vary.)

jar with plant matter and then pour in the strongest alcohol you can find. It's easy to find more specific recipes in herbal books, but that will usually do the trick. This time, I found a formula that called for a mixture of one part plant matter to two parts liquid solvent, which was proscribed to be 50 percent alcohol. To make it, I poured the 190-proof vodka over the roots just a little more than halfway to the top of the glass jar and let tap water fill the rest. Then I screwed the lid on the jar and left it alone for six weeks in a dark cupboard. When I came back to look at it later, the alcohol had extracted the berberine, resulting in a dark golden brown liquid.

※

It came in handy when I awoke one day with tonsils the size of strawberries, and a fever, and swollen lymph glands in my neck. My old standbys have long been sleep and water, so I tried those for a day, but the symptoms of infection didn't relent. I thought I probably had strep throat, which meant it would be a perfect time to try the Oregon grape root tincture.

I took the jar down from the cupboard and placed it on my kitchen counter. As I unscrewed the lid, I noticed that the part of me that had internalized messages from my childhood felt uncomfortable with this. I thought, *Who am I to make my own medicine? Who am I to know when to take it?* I was raised to believe that when we feel ill, we must see a doctor to tell us what's wrong, and then we must go to a pharmacist to get curative drugs made by highly educated scientists who have a deep understanding of biochemistry.

Usually, the drugs are mysterious to me and have a list of ingredients that are unpronounceable by all but those in the medical establishment. As a patient I have felt disempowered by this dynamic and utterly dependent. In making and taking my own medicine, I felt powerful and self-sufficient—surprisingly radical, subversive even.

If I look at myself in the context of human history, it is strange that I should have felt uncomfortable taking herbal medicine at all, because people have been relying on it since before we were even *Homo sapiens*. Archaeologists found yarrow—the plant Ariel brewed beer with, and which not only stops bleeding externally but is also used internally as a cold remedy—in a sixty-thousand-year-old Neanderthal cave.[24] Herbal medicine is used in all cultures in all parts of the world and remains hugely popular in the Chinese medical tradition today. In the West, records of herbal medicine go back to Pedanius Dioscorides, a first-century Greek botanist who served the army of the Roman Emperor Nero. His five-volume encyclopedia of medicinal plants, *De Materia Medica,* was the most influential book on the subject for fifteen hundred years.[25]

Even animals of other species, such as bears, take medicinal herbs in the wild when they don't feel well. This

24. There is evidence that *Homo sapiens* lived concurrently with Neanderthals; scholars argue about whether our species may have interbred with them. Given the existence of *Maxim* magazine, it seems likely.

25. The earliest known record of medical writing is a Sumerian recipe for a topical paste made of beer from 2100 BC.

phenomenon is called zoopharmacognosy, and a number of researchers have studied and documented it. In 1972 a field researcher in Tanzania watched a chimpanzee dubbed "Hugo" forage a grassland plant there called *Aspilia rudis,* which was surprising, because it wasn't part of his usual diet; it is rough, sharp, and unpleasant to eat.

"Hugo had not only sought it out but he'd also eaten the leaves in a particular way, carefully folding them up concertina-style and holding them briefly in his mouth before swallowing. From the way he was grimacing, it looked just as if he was taking an old-fashioned medicine . . . [Researchers found that] *Aspilia* leaves were used by local herbalists for stomach upsets and that they contained chemicals that were both antibacterial and attacked gut parasites. What's more, other chimps were seen occasionally eating from nineteen other plants that also had rough leaves, in the same way. The leaves were excreted whole and, when examined closely, tiny nodular worms that infect the gut could be seen wriggling on the barbs on the leaf surface."[26]

This kind of thing is old news for indigenous cultures across the world, whose medicine stories tell of learning about herbs by observing animal behavior.

꽃

26. This is taken from a story by Jerome Burne published in *The Guardian* in 2002 about the book *Wild Health: How Animals Keep Themselves Well and What We Can Learn From Them* by Cindy Engel.

Outlaws

I squeezed a medicine dropper into the jar of Oregon grape root tincture and gently eased my pinch-hold on the tip until the golden brown liquid filled the glass tube all the way to the top. I released it on my tongue. It was very, very bitter, so I decided to put it in hot tea with honey instead. I crushed dried lemon balm, *Melissa officinalis,* and rosemary, both of which I had gathered within two blocks of my house, and put them in a tea ball. Both herbs are in the mint family, and mints are antimicrobial, so I reasoned that they, combined with a little honey, which is also antimicrobial, would be good adjuncts to the tincture.

I had never taken natural medicine before, at least not overtly. Certainly I had used medicines derived from plants without realizing it. Many modern drugs are made from plants. Aspirin was originally made from the salicin found in meadowsweet, *Spiraea ulmaria.* The painkillers morphine and codeine are chemical compounds found in opium poppies, *Papaver somniferum,* a Traditional Chinese Medicine. Wild cherry cough drops used to have actual wild cherry bark in them, a remedy for coughs. Still, I figured that if the herbs worked, they would probably be subtle and slower-acting than the doctor-prescribed antibiotics I was used to taking.

I called Emily and asked her if there were any herbs I might want to add in, and she said I should go get cleavers, *Galium aparine,* to address the swollen lymph glands in my neck. I knew exactly where to look. The alley behind my apartment building was full of it. Cleavers could double as herbal jewelry, because it has little hairs attached to it that stick to you like Velcro. You can wear it as a lapel pin if you want, no accessories required. It's also known as bedstraw. Animals build nests with the plant, and books say people used to stuff it in their bedding as well.

I pulled up a handful of cleavers and went upstairs to my kitchen to rinse the greens and chop them up. Then I put them in a glass jar and filled it with cold tap water, in accordance with Emily's directions. I let it stand overnight. The following morning the water in the jar was a soft grass color. I drank the whole thing, and I rather liked it. It reminded me of cucumber water.

By that evening, I felt tremendously better. By the following morning, I was back to normal. My tonsils had shrunk down, my neck glands were no longer swollen, and there was no fever. I was surprised at how quickly the herbs worked: In two days, I was healthy again. It cost me nothing except for the alcohol. Anyone could do this, no health insurance required.

When I told my friends how well the plant medicine had worked for me, they texted me when they got sick to ask if they could try my tinctures, too. Many of them do not have health insurance and cannot afford to go to the doctor. I happily gave them little bottles of my Oregon grape tincture and tea herbs to take with it. I didn't ask for money at the time because I liked giving the medicine as a present. Each time they got sick and took the tincture, my friends got better within two to three days—and saved hundreds of dollars. Two people took Oregon grape for strep throat. Another person gave it to her son when he came down with a high fever. A woman I knew at the local dog park took my Oregon grape root tincture to kick a persistent cold virus. It worked. Then she gave it to her Labrador mix when the dog got sick from drinking contaminated river water. That worked, too. Veterinarians say that dogs can take most of the same herbs people do, and for the same reasons—they just need smaller doses. Everyone took two droppers full three times a day— except the dog, who took a smaller dose—and recovered within two to three days without any side effects.

When I saw how effective plant medicine could be, I ordered a bunch of how-to books and started making many different kinds. I tinctured stinging nettle as an allergy remedy, elder flower for the flu, *Usnea* lichen for pneumonia, bearberry, *Uva ursi,* for urinary tract infections, California poppy, *Eschscholzia californica,* for insomnia, cleavers as a lymph tonic, and lemon balm for worry. I rarely got sick, but I liked making the medicine, and I especially liked being able to share it with friends and family when they needed it. At the dog park, people started calling me "the neighborhood herbalist."

Legally speaking, this was interesting territory. It is legal to make your own herbal medicine and share it with people, in the same way that it's cool to make your own blackberry jam and share it, but you have to be careful how you term what you do, because it is illegal to diagnose or treat disease without a medical license, and there is no medical licensing for herbalists.

"Herbalists come up with a lot of verbal gymnastics for this. Whereas you're not allowed to diagnose disease, you are allowed to promote health. If I say, 'This herb is good for your lung functioning, and it's good for helping you take nice deep breaths that aren't encumbered by lots of phlegm,' I haven't diagnosed any disease. But if I said, 'I think you have asthma, and I'll give you something to treat your asthma,' I could get in a lot of trouble," said Erico Schleicher, who teaches herbal medicine at the Elderberry School of Botanical Medicine in Portland, which he cofounded.

I was acting as a folk herbalist, essentially. By making local medicine in a city and giving it to my community, I was joining a small but diverse subculture of urban healers all over the world. In New York City, people from the Dominican Republic and Puerto Rico give each other herbal medicine. In London, Colombian immigrants do it, too.

❧

I wondered: If herbal medicine works this well, why did it go underground in the first place? I knew I was asking a big question with many answers. Medical historian Jacalyn Duffy sees it as part of a broader shift that began in the mid-nineteenth century. Until then, a doctor's role was primarily to diagnose and predict the outcome of your ailment, and to alleviate suffering if possible. This was the era of virulent epidemics and heroic medicine, when doctors prescribed poisonous metals such as mercury and arsenic, because the prevailing belief was that remedies should be more vicious than diseases in order to defeat them. This approach killed many patients, and so people sought out an array of alternative options. They went to holistic practitioners, wise woman herbalists in their families, and priests for spiritual healing.

Three major developments turned the tide in doctors' favor and encouraged patients to trust them: the invention of anesthesia and antisepsis in the mid-nineteenth century, which made surgery much less painful and risky; the advent of antibiotic drugs in the 1930s and 1940s, which showed that technology could make powerful cures; and lobbying efforts by the American Medical Association. The AMA was founded in 1847 partly as a professional lobby to protect doctors' interests. One of the ways it sought to do this was by undermining and eliminating the holistic competition, which was considerable: Around 1900, one out of every four doctor visits in the United States was to someone other than a regular physician. By aligning standard medical schools with well-funded universities, and by applying political pressure to influence the required curriculum for state licensing of medical schools, the AMA gradually created an allopathic hegemony. Today, there are very few alternative medical colleges, and there's no such thing as a licensed herbalist in America.

7
Erico of the Herbs

Erico is one of those baby-faced folks whose age could reside in either of two decades. He won't say which, even if pressed. I tried asking directly one time, but he just smiled at me and made daggers of his eyes before changing the subject. The most I could get out of him is that his dreadlocks, which are mid-back length, have been hanging there for at least fifteen years. "I'll tell you how I got them," he offered.

"Okay," I said. "How?"

"I spent a summer in the woods and forgot to bring a hairbrush."

He has a lot of stories like this, vagabond-type stories that start with him living out of a backpack and end with him doing something on a whim. There's that time he tried to walk from New Mexico to California by himself through the desert and got lost and ran out of water and had to turn back. There's that time he went hitchhiking out of Ohio after he got his bachelor's degree in anthropology. And then there's the one about how he was wandering around

Albuquerque one day when he just happened to poke his head into Michael R.S. Moore's famous Southwest School of Botanical Medicine.

"I walked in and I was like, 'This is what I want to do.' I knew it pretty instantly. It was like getting struck by lightning," he said.

"Have you gotten struck by lightning?" I asked.

"Only metaphorically," he admitted. "I've never been struck by lightning, touch wood."

We were standing in his office, a room with tall wooden bookcases filled floor to ceiling with titles I expected to see, such as *Stalking the Wild Asparagus, Chinese Medical Herbology and Pharmacology,* and Moore's *Medicinal Plants of the Pacific West*, as well as a few I didn't anticipate, such as a poetry book by Patti Smith and a field guide to insects with a praying mantis on the cover. He was particularly excited about the latter.

"I figured out what it is that's so appealing about praying mantises," Erico said, beaming. "It's that they have necks!" He stuck his head out awkwardly in an attempt to imitate a mantis. "If you look at them, they'll turn their head and look at you. Ants don't do that."

He's full of random insights like that, which is why I came over that day. I wanted to get his take on my big question. When we were comfortably seated on his couch in his living room, I asked him, "Why, in mainstream America, is herbal medicine seen as something that's weird and shaky and unreliable? Why did *I* think it would be ineffective?"

He was quiet for a moment, contemplating my question. "Our culture has moved, since the fifties or so, away from contact with plants and dirt, away from recognizing that plants are an essential part of our lives as a species. People are afraid of earthy things. They live in sterilized antiseptic homes now, or on the fourteenth floor of an apartment building. I read this story that the average child can't recognize even ten species of trees but knows over a thousand corporate logos, which means that the knowledge of plants is probably at an all-time low."

Erico poured me some chamomile-mint-rose-petal tea he had made. "One of the classes I teach," he said, "starts with trying to get people to recognize our dependency on plants. Some things are so ubiquitous in our culture that people don't even recognize that they're plants anymore."

"Like what?" I asked.

"The best example for Americans is mint. Everything is mint flavored, and nobody realizes that they're dealing with a plant. Multiple times a day, we owe the taste in our mouth to a plant. Black pepper is on every table in America, but no one gets to see the plant because it doesn't grow here, it grows tropically. And coffee and chocolate."

"Oh, those *are* plants, aren't they?" I said.

"Oh, those *are* plants, aren't they?" he said, mocking me. "They're plants. Coffee's a plant. Tea is a plant. Chocolate—cacao—is a plant. Even the things that are refined to the point of being white powder, like sugar, come from plants."

Erico lives in a cozy one-story bungalow with a blue exterior. His medicine room has stacks of plastic bins containing dried herbs and cabinets filled with dark brown bottles containing tinctures. On top of one cabinet is a glass jar of chopped up redroot, *Ceanothus velutinus.* Across the room on top of another shelving unit he had osha root, *Ligusticum porteri,* in a plastic bag, which he invited me to smell. It was delightful. He had racks of screens drying alder tree catkins, yellow dock root chopped into pieces, dandelion, magnolia buds,[27] some stinging nettle, and artichoke leaf.

"Is it true there are herbal antibiotics?" I asked, wondering if that was the right terminology for Oregon grape root.

"Sure, there are plants with antimicrobial properties," Erico said. "Antibiotic literally means antilife. All of the antibiotic pharmaceutical drugs used in conventional medicine are basically antibacterial. The other things that we need to be able to fight sometimes are viruses and fungi. The plant world has to deal with its own invasive microbes and often comes up with chemicals to defend itself. So a lot of the things we make use of are plants' own defense mechanisms against microbes. We live in an area where one of the most important trees is Western red cedar. And the Pacific Northwest is a place with a lot of dampness, fungi, a lot of mold. The traditional people figured out who knows how many thousands of years ago that cedar wood doesn't rot. Cedar leaves don't rot. And they built things out of it that were going to be exposed to a lot of water—like boats, like clothes—and as a plant medicine, it is a topical antifungal. You can make footbaths from a strong tea of the leaves; some people extract the essential oils. It's a strong antifungal, for a plant."

27. The fragrant ones can be inhaled via steam as a remedy for sinus issues.

We went outside to walk around in Erico's garden. We picked bright orange calendula flowers and blue borage blossoms and ate them, and then we strolled around to the backyard, where we came to a stand of bleeding heart, *Dicentra formosa,* a plant that has narcotic properties.[28] I watched a bumblebee buzz around its delicate, bell-shaped pink flowers. I asked him if there were any philosophical differences in how professional herbalists like him view medicine, compared with how conventional doctors do.

"Almost all over-the-counter drugs are suppressive; their intention is to suppress symptoms so that you can keep going to work," he said. "But many of the things that happen to us when we're sick happen for a good reason. A lot of the older herbalism, and a lot of traditional American and European and Greek medicine, were oriented toward strengthening the body's reactions. This is the root of holistic medicine."

"What about a fever? How is a fever good?" I asked.

"A fever is a wonderful reaction that the body has to cook out a pathogen," Erico said. "All of the old herbs that people used for colds and flus and fevers were diaphoretic herbs—Chinese medicine says, 'Release the exterior.' In European and American traditions, these are things like elderflower and mint and ginger and yarrow flowers,

---

28. Many herbalists consider bleeding heart dangerous and rarely use it; Erico is one of them.

herbs that help the body open up the pores, sweat a little bit and expel pathogens."

He continued, "When the illness finds its way past the outer defenses, the usual place it goes first is either the lungs or the stomach. If it goes to the lungs, the immune system wants to produce lots of phlegm and expectorate this stuff. White blood cells are able to move around more easily in good quality mucus. You want to be making phlegm and expelling phlegm. Or if you have a cat scratch on your hand, the temperature of the infection site locally can get up to 110 degrees. That's inflammation—it's the body's attempt to mobilize lots of energy and local blood and flood it with everything the immune system needs and cook out the infectious agent with heat. It's all supposed to happen this way. So all of these immune system reactions are exactly what we want to support."

Just as a forager eats by making the best of what nature already plants, an herbalist heals by embracing what nature already does.

8

Doggy Herbalism

My dog, a thirty-pound Chihuahua-terrier mix named Petunia, came down with a cold last winter. She couldn't walk more than a few feet without sneezing. It was funny to watch but obviously uncomfortable for her, so I decided to try some doggy herbalism. "Petunia, do you want a cookie?" I asked.

She looked at me expectantly with her adorable almond-shaped eyes gone wide and hopeful. She followed me into the kitchen, her nails click-clacking on the linoleum tile. I opened the cabinet where I keep her treats and she sat at attention, her gaze intent on me. "This is a special one," I said to her, as I took out a treat with a hole in the top of it. While she watched, I squeezed yarrow flower tincture onto it and disguised the flavor with a dab of peanut butter. I gave it to her and she sniffed it apprehensively, seemingly unsure about the alcohol smell, so I added more and more peanut butter until she was convinced that the weird scent was worth ignoring. I repeated the dose a few more times in the next couple days and she stopped sneezing.

Another time, Petunia curled up in my bed, as she often does at night, and I noticed that her heartbeat seemed irregular against my feet. I took her to the vet for a diagnosis, and he confirmed that Petunia had a mild arrhythmia. Fortunately, I knew that there was a large hawthorn tree at the dog park, and I knew that hawthorn is a remedy for heart problems, so I encouraged her to eat the berries. At first she was reluctant; the dogs there tend to ignore the red fruit on the ground even though it's perfectly edible. I smushed them up and called them "cookies," feeding them to her as a reward to get her interested. I showed her that I was eating them, too, and then she became so excited that she stopped playing with the other dogs and just wanted to eat berries. This continued for months. What happened next was really interesting—the other dogs saw her eating the berries and copied her behavior. Now the squirrels have some competition, because there are several dogs who act like vacuum cleaners.

ॐ

Just the other day, I noticed Petunia had a scrape on her shoulder and another at the top of her nose. She had pink skin where fur used to be. It wasn't bleeding or infected, just a little bit raw. Maybe she got scratched in the bushes when we went hiking.

"I've got a remedy for your problems," I told Petunia. "I'm going to make you a comfrey salve."

Comfrey, *Symphytum officinale,* is a common weed in the borage family that helps skin regenerate very quickly;

it's used topically for wound healing on scrapes and burns and cuts.[29] I had comfrey in my possession already because one of the dog park denizens grows her own vegetables and has a very big garden, and one of the weeds in her garden was comfrey, which, when she told me that, I gladly took off her hands. I dried it and mostly forgot about it for a couple months, until that moment.

Since Petunia had an urgent need, I decided to go with a super-speedy method of salve-making. Most people go with the slow-infusion style, which is where you pour a medicinal herb into a jar and fill it with oil and keep it near a heater for weeks or even months to let the herb infuse. The quick version uses alcohol. I crushed the comfrey leaves and put them in a jar and poured grain alcohol over them until it was three-quarters full, and then I added just a splash of water to the rest and covered it. I read how to do this in Michael Moore's book *Medicinal Plants of the Pacific West*. It's called a "maceration," and it helps break down the plant and extract the medicine much faster. You can let the jar sit anywhere from a couple hours to overnight. Just half an hour after I mixed the alcohol and the herbs together, the water in the jar had turned a vibrant emerald green.

Before I could add it to almond oil and beeswax to make the salve, I needed some small jars, so I went to the grocery store and bought baby food. It's pretty cheap at fifty cents

29. It is important to disinfect any wound before applying comfrey because it works so well that if there's any bacteria caught inside, it can heal the skin at the surface and trap it, potentially causing an infection. For the same reason, comfrey is generally not used on deep wounds.

each. I chose mashed banana and sweet potato off the shelf because they're delicious. Maybe only parents and herbalists know this, but baby food is way underrated.

I washed out the jars when I was done eating and left them to dry overnight. In the morning, I poured the grass-green tincture with a little bit of the leaf inside it into a blender, using the ratio of seven parts almond oil to one part tincture and herb. I let it run for several minutes, until the sides of the blender were warm, and then I put it in a Crock-Pot on my counter with melted beeswax. I stirred the combination until it all melted together and poured it into the glass jars. Once cooled, it had the consistency of soft lip balm, and a bright chartreuse color.

I swabbed my finger in the green stuff and applied it to Petunia's nose and shoulder. She kept trying to lick it off her nose. I didn't notice an instant change, but her scrapes seemed to get better after a few days.

9

The Tree That Slays the Flu

An old friend leaned her shoulder in the doorway of my kitchen. I had just given her a tour of my apothecary, showing her my shelves full of tincture bottles and drying herbs. Now I was standing at the counter, rolling chocolate truffle balls I had made out of coconut butter and agave in cinnamon powder. The two of us were eating them and catching up.

"I want to learn how to do what you do," my friend said.

"It's easy," I told her. "We can go pick dandelion outside today and make a detoxifying tincture. You're into doing cleanses, so you'll like it. We just need to buy some alcohol first."

I shut the door behind us and we set off to walk the half a dozen or so blocks between my place and the liquor store. We were almost there when I noticed a striking purple tree. Its deep burgundy leaves and pink flowers draped over a parked car in the street.

"Check this out," I said, walking toward it. "Elderberry!"

I knew how to identify the tree because the leaves are arranged in groups of five to nine leaflets and the flowers hang in disc-like clusters with tiny, star-shaped blossoms. My friend and I stuck our noses in them, devouring their perfumed scent with glee.

"I've heard of elderberry," my friend said, "but I didn't know what it looked like."

Even if she had, she might not have been familiar with this one, which was one of the forty different ornamental varieties bred from the black elderberry, *Sambucus nigra*,[30] a shrub that grows up to almost nineteen feet tall with black fruit. The other two most common species are blue, *Sambucus cerulea*, a tree up to almost forty feet tall that grows in dry, open habitats and has dark blue berries; and red, *Sambucus racemosa*, which is prolific in the forests, meadows, and stream banks around here and has red or orange berries. All varieties have edible fruit, though the red ones are not popular because they have to be cooked first to neutralize toxins. The blue and black are used for jams, syrups, and wines.

"Let's forget about the dandelion and harvest these elder flowers instead," I said. I like the element of surprise in foraging, the adventure of discovery, and the experiences that remind me that living in nature means being adaptive and resourceful: *carpe diem*. "We can use the paper bag they'll give us at the liquor store to collect them. Then we'll have herbal flu medicine."

30. The Latin word *Sambucus* is similar to the Greek word "sambuke," which refers to an ancient musical instrument. Even today some people hollow out the branches and play them as flutes. They can be blowguns for poison darts, too.

When I had come down with body aches and fatigue a year prior, I traded a bottle of my Oregon grape root tincture for another herbalist's elderberry extract. I put a few droppers full of her sweet, wine-colored tincture in tea and drank it three times that day and three times the next. By the second evening, I felt drastically better. This was no fluke: In a study of Norwegian people who were sick with the flu published in the *Journal of International Medical Research*, 90 percent of those who took elderberry extract were back to health within three days. The control group was given a placebo and had the flu twice as long. The medicine is found in both the flower and the berry.

As my friend and I pinched the flower clusters off the tree, I warned her to be careful not to grab anything else. "The leaves and twigs have compounds in them that produce cyanide. All parts of this plant are potentially toxic except for the flowers and the fruits they'll turn into," I said.

Back at my place, we pulled the flower clusters apart, filled glass jars with them, poured Everclear halfway to the top, and added tap water to the rest. "This is amazing," my friend said. "I had no idea that medicine grows on the street like this."

It's true. Everywhere we look, we see useful plants. The Earth is full of medicine for the people, and it's available free of charge.

PART THREE:

The Revolution Tastes Like Blackberry

10

Margot Berlin

It turns out that if you post a "free weeding" ad on craigslist, people send more responses than you can handle. I tried this once on a puddle-filled spring day, requesting only that the winning yard be free of pesticides and any other known contaminants. "This is a win-win proposition," I wrote. "You get rid of unwanted weeds, and I get to eat them."

I got a lot of replies, but I was most intrigued by the one from a woman with a name like a German burlesque performer: Margot Berlin. She said she lived about two miles away in a gang-infested neighborhood on a street that has more potholes than the moon has craters. I rode my bicycle to her address, where I found a dark purple house behind a chain-link fence guarded by some very excitedly barking and yipping dogs. One looked like an overweight golden retriever; the other was a strange-looking little guy with a brindle coat. "This is Lucius," Margot said. "He's half monkey and half Yoda, and acts like he's mostly gargoyle. Sometimes I think he was jettisoned from space."

When I first set eyes on her, I thought Margot had a strong resemblance to the actress Helena Bonham Carter, with dark brown eyes, pale skin, and—this is unlike that actress— long wavy hair as silver as an elderly matron's. It was a stunning juxtaposition against her smooth skin. "Welcome," she said, showing me to a large patch of weeds in her side yard. "Have at it."

I took a digging tool out of my backpack and got to work right away. My trowel sliced easily into the damp dirt. I wedged it diagonally toward the dandelion root and pushed down on the handle to send gooey mud to the surface, freeing the roots I wanted. My fingers were covered in slimy soil, but I didn't mind that at all. In fact I noticed that it felt really, really good to touch the earth.

Margot walked out of her house and brought me the best cup of coffee I'd ever had while I dug up the roots, and when I was finished, she invited me inside to see her paintings. She told me that she was a recovering agoraphobic, and she was happier than anything to have a visitor.

The two of us hit it off, and pretty soon I was coming over to her house to hang out all the time. She'd light up a joint of medical marijuana, fully legal in Oregon with her state-issued card, while I smoked a hand-rolled spliff of fully legal wild herbs harvested from around town. I made them with a blend of dried mullein leaves, *Verbascum thapsus,* which has a nutty taste and a cooling, fluffy, smooth texture; the light purple flowers of Russian sage, *Perouskia atriplicifolia,* a menthol-flavored ornamental plant native to Pakistan that happens to contain thujone, one constituent of absinthe; lemon balm, a mild sedative with a citrus flavor; and vanilla leaf, *Achlys triphylla,* to add a subtle vanilla flavor. I had picked the mullein from Jason's garden, snipped feral lemon balm from an alleyway, gathered the Russian sage flowers from along Alberta Street, and found the vanilla leaf in a local forest. I had dried the plants in my apartment, hanging them upside down in bunches from a nylon cord I strung between two shelves in my office. I used paper clips to make hooks and attached them to wire twisty ties I wrapped around the bundles. Once dried, I stored them in glass jars. I gave Margot one and labeled it the "#1 Best Super Relax Happy Time Smoke Mix." When I felt like inhaling it, I crushed the plants up by hand, mixed them together, and smoked them out of glass pipes or rolled them in tobacco papers. I like the way they smell and the gentle way the mullein makes the smoke feel in my lungs. I've never been a tobacco smoker—the smell repels me—and pot just makes me anxious. My blend of wild plants is not as intoxicating as that, but it does have a noticeably relaxing effect, which is to be expected, given that lemon balm has anti-anxiety effects. As Margot puts it, the blend offers "feel-goodness."

※

Margot dazzled me with her quirky short stories that I couldn't believe she had never published. I brought her jars of my homemade stinging nettle pesto, which she savored. I gave her some of my Oregon grape root tincture when her son got sick, and he got well very quickly. When she was diagnosed with an arrhythmia, I made her hawthorn medicine for her heart. There was a hawthorn tree at the local dog park, I clipped the freshly flowering twigs into a glass jar and filled it with brandy for her.

I like how foraging can build relationships like that.

One of the best times I had with Margot was when we went to gather blackberries on her street in August. As soon as I walked up the steps to her place, Lucius went berserk, as he often does, darting around the living room. "He's going right back down the mouth of the Gypsy curse that spawned him," Margot said, wrangling him off the top of the couch.

She was wearing cowboy boots and a floppy black sunhat to which she had affixed a dead squirrel's face, switching its eyeballs out for red Czechoslovakian crystals. She had put new crow feathers on her altar, which was already strewn with dried rose petals, a dried snake skin she'd ordered on the Internet, and some black hen's feet. She is Choctaw, African-American, German, and Irish, and though she grew up Catholic, her ritual practice is based on HooDoo, a form of African-American folk magic. She calls her version Provda, which is also the name of a language she is inventing. It sounds like Russian.

"Did you feel like English doesn't have enough words or something?" I asked her.

"Well, it's kind of similar to German, where you have a single word that encompasses the whole of an idea," she said. "I created this language because there were no words to adequately express my grief over love. In this particular case, to love someone as much as I did and have them be so fucking terrible for you."

"I understand," I said.

"In Provda it's the same word for grief as for love," she said.

⚘

We put down the glasses of iced coffee we were drinking and went out into the yard, where Margot put Lucius on his leash. It was after five o'clock already, but the sun was shining hot and bright. I still don't quite understand how things work this way, my being from the East Coast and all, but somehow in Portland the day gets hotter as it goes on instead of peaking around noon like it does in New Jersey.

"Look at that huge burdock," Margot said, pointing toward the road.

"That?" I asked, following her line of sight to a six-foot-tall plant with a thick red stalk. "Ah, that's not burdock, that's pokeweed," I said. "It's very toxic. It's gonna make berries. In the South people eat the very young leaves, but you have to boil them in two or three changes of water to get out the toxins. It can be lethal otherwise."

"I don't think I'll ever be hungry enough to try it," Margot said.

Pokeweed, *Phytolacca americana*, is also known as poke sallet. No one eats it raw and leaves feeling good, despite the resemblance of "sallet" to the word "salad." It has other neat uses though. The fermented juice of pokeberries—they stain a dark purple-red—was used to write the US Constitution. Pokeweed is also being studied as a treatment for leukemia.

I followed Margot around the side of her house, where she showed me a stunning flower on a bittersweet vine,

Solanum dulcumara, which is very poisonous to eat but also has anti-cancer compounds in it. Next to the vine was a small blackberry plant with beautiful black-purple berries glistening in the sun. "Can I have one?" I asked.

Margot plucked a berry and handed it to me. It was so ripe it squished in her fingers and juice spilled out. "Oh, I just killed it," she said. "You can have its bloody remains."

With colanders in hand, we made our way across her yard toward the big patch of blackberries growing across the street, where we were going to have ourselves a harvest. As we passed a wooden sign painted with the words, EXPECT A MIRACLE, I pretended to narrate the scene aloud, as if we were in a documentary. "The sign is reflecting Margot's decidedly optimistic outlook on life, despite her recent problems in love," I said.

"I wouldn't call them problems, I would call them learning experiences," she said. "And I got a lot of art out of it."

"See, that's what I'm saying," I said.

❧

Margot closed the gate behind us as we made our way across the unpaved dirt road with the potholes in it. She calls her road "country in the city," and it does feel like that, especially with her chickens running around the yard. Margot has a bit of the farm girl in her. She grew up in a rural town called Lebanon, Oregon, where foraging was part of daily life, as was hunting for food. Her family and their neighbors would gather fruit at u-pick farms together and help each other with rural chores like baling hay, and if someone had a fruit tree, the neighbors would come over and help pick it so it didn't go to waste. She remembers gleaners going through the farm fields, too, and distributing what they got to the poor, something that now happens in Portland and other cities through coordinated efforts of nonprofits like the Portland Fruit Tree Project.

The blackberry cluster we were going to pick from was not a mere bramble but instead a wall of thorns at least twenty feet tall and at least as wide. Margot assured me that the neighbor who owns the land where these blackberries live doesn't spray any chemicals on them because she knows people from all over the neighborhood come by and pick them.

I leaned in to get my first berry and got poked with a sharp thorn immediately. "Damn it," I cursed.

"I think the key with picking blackberries is if you get stuck, don't panic," Margot said.

"Keep calm and carry on?" I offered.

"Well, you know, graciously accept your fate and then let go," she said.

"Is that Buddhist?" I asked.

"It should be. Maybe that'll be my next thing: create a sect of Buddhism," she said.

The berries stained my fingers purple as I pulled them off the canes. After ten minutes, we had just two cups worth. "It doesn't seem like very much," I said.

"When I was younger, my grandma was freakishly fast at picking strawberries to make money," Margot told me, "even after she lost her fingers."

Margot Berlin

"I'm sorry, what was that? 'Even after she lost her fingers'?"

"Yeah, I think it was my cow, Honey. She had a rope around Honey's neck and Honey bolted for some reason, and the rope got tangled around my grandma's fingers, and the cow and her fingers went on one side of the tree and she went on the other. One of them we couldn't find—we don't know if a dog ran off with it or something."

"Oh my," I said. "That sounds like a terrible accident."

"They were able to sew one of the fingers back on, and she went right back out there with a handsaw taking down trees, but then it turned black and they had to take it back off."

"Is it wrong that I'm laughing at your grandmother's misfortune?" I asked.

"Oh, it's totally not wrong—that shit's funny. You can't really see it in a lot of pictures, but she'd always say to my father, 'I salute you,' like this, and it looked like she was giving him the bird."

⁂

The more time we spent picking, the more efficient we seemed to get at it, and yet I never felt bored. It was very pleasant, relaxing even, and I noticed my mood turning increasingly playful and light. Environmental psychologists have documented this phenomenon of nature-as-mood-booster in numerous studies. It is established fact that seeing or being near vegetation improves one's emotional well-being, physiological health, and attention span. One study found that mood elevation occurs for most people within thirty minutes of entering an urban park.

We rinsed the berries under cold tap water in Margot's sink. They were a beautiful color, like garnet. A tiny white spider crawled out as we sprayed the fruit, and Margot carefully picked it up by a strand of web to which it was attached and deftly dropped it out a sideways sliding window to safety. "Excuse me, spider," she said.

I was glad to see a jar of cottonwood salve on her coffee table in the living room. We had made it together a few months prior. I had the ingredients on hand because my boyfriend at the time had given me a gift of cottonwood buds that he had picked in a riparian park. Cottonwood trees, *Populus balsamifera,* also called balsam poplar or balm of Gilead, grow in wet meadows and along rivers and lakes from Alaska to Southern California and across the top half of North America as far south as Virginia. Harvest time is late winter and early spring, when the bright orange-red buds are sticky with resin. The resin is antibacterial and anti-inflammatory, and if you infuse the buds into olive oil, and then mix the oil with melted beeswax, as we did, then you can have an antiseptic salve to apply to cuts and burns. "Can I put a little of this cottonwood salve on my blackberry scratches?" I asked.

"Of course," she said. She unscrewed the lid and handed me the jar, and I swiped some yellow beeswax with my finger. It had a consistency like lip balm. I applied it to the scratches on my hands. By the next morning, I couldn't see them, let alone feel them.

11

Dime-size God

Margot stood around the side of a bakery and waited for me to come out with two white paper cookie bags. She picked a rose and smelled it as traffic drove by on the busy street. I asked her to meet me here at a stand of amaranth I've had my eye on. It was late summer, and we were next to an island of weeds, mostly feral fennel. The grass was straw colored, all dried out from the summer heat. Neither of us had done this before. We put the bags right up to the drier, rust-colored seed heads and shook them and tapped the seeds into the bags; the greener seed heads took a little more nudging and rubbing to get the seeds loose.

"They're beautiful," Margot said, looking into the bag. The seeds are black and dark brown-red and very, very small, like poppy seeds, except shinier.

We had collected fewer of them than the spiny seed husks. We separated the two by putting the mixture into our palms and blowing gently: The beige husks and debris blew away and the seeds stuck to our skin.

"I read that amaranth seeds are like quinoa, but now that I see it, I don't think it's that practical an idea," I said. After half an hour of harvesting and separating the seeds from the chaff, we had a tablespoon of seeds between the two of us.

"Maybe if we had Aztec skills it'd be easier," Margot said.

"The seeds might have been a lot bigger because they were cultivated back then," I said.

Amaranth seeds, *Amaranthus* spp., are 15 percent protein. If you manage to gather enough, you can roast them or boil them like rice. Now a lowly weed very few people ever recognize, this plant was once the staple food of the Aztecs. In one of his books, forager-author Steve Brill writes that the Aztecs used to roast the seeds, mix them with honey, and then mold them into the shape of a war deity that they ate in a ceremony.

"Are you ready to eat some war god?" I asked Margot.

"Tiny war god," she said. "Dime-size god."

I walked into the kitchen to get a frying pan to toast the seeds in. Margot came with me, blowing on the seeds to get any last bit of debris out of the mix. We put them in the pan and turned the flame to medium-low.

I thought of how these seeds link us across time and space to ancient agrarians. Researchers believe amaranth was first domesticated six thousand years ago in Central America. In the eastern United States, American Indians started farming about 2500 BC with sunflower and goosefoot, *Chenopodium* spp., a close relative of amaranth that is also known as lamb's quarters. In central and southern Mexico, people switched over to farming in 3500 BC, starting with corn, beans, and squash.

Dime-size God

In other parts of the world, farming began ten thousand years ago during a period of climate change, an increase in population densities, and a decrease in the availability of large animals to hunt. It's not clear which of these factors were causes and which were effects; academics argue about it.

I once assumed that farming replaced foraging because it represented a sort of evolutionary leap in food security and, above all, a better quality of life. Then I read that modern hunter-gatherer cultures actually enjoy a higher quality of life than those of us in agricultural societies, especially in terms of health. With their unprocessed, whole-food diets and active lifestyles, people who hunt and gather rarely develop high blood pressure, high cholesterol, obesity, or insulin resistance. A study in the *Journal of Physiology* found the rate of diabetes in hunter-gatherer societies is 1.1 percent, while in the United States the rate was 8.3 percent in 2011, as reported by the American Diabetes Association. Studies on hunter-gatherer societies in the twentieth century showed them to be "generally free of the signs and symptoms" of heart disease, as analyzed by a report in the *European Journal of Clinical Nutrition*. Cancers of the stomach and breast among hunter-gatherers are virtually nonexistent.

Hunter-gatherers typically work fewer hours and have more leisure time than those of us in industrialized societies, too. When anthropologist Richard B. Lee lived among the San people in the Kalahari Desert, he found that adults worked only twelve to fifteen hours per week. Other researchers have reported similar statistics elsewhere, though some quibble over whether those figures include the time it takes to process wild food, which sometimes can be quite substantial, as well as what exactly constitutes work. Is hunting and gathering your food really work at all? In America we tend to think of berry picking, hunting, and fishing as leisure activities. We do it on the weekends, for fun.

The common myth that life as a hunter-gatherer is one of hardship may have originated in part with that oft-repeated but ill-conceived "nasty, brutish, and short" quip Thomas Hobbes, the English philosopher, wrote in 1651 to describe what life would be like if we lived in a "state of nature" without centralized government. Hobbes believed that people are violent savages at heart and that government by absolute monarchy is the best way to ensure peace. The implication— incorrect, we now know—was that hunter-gatherers must suffer nightmarish lives.

Complicating matters, early Euro-American anthropologists narcissistically assumed that they represented the pinnacle of human potential, and that cultures that did not share their model of civilization were therefore stunted. When anthropology first developed as a discipline in the nineteenth century, it was heavily influenced by Enlightenment ideas about progress. Author and anthropologist Robert L. Kelly explains this fallacious early thinking in his book, *The Foraging Spectrum:*

"Just as God could be ranked above the whole of humanity, so could cultures and ethnic groups be ranked in their respective degrees of perfection. The history of humanity was seen as operating according to universal, natural laws that led to the moral development of people, and that was evidenced by the increasing subjugation of nature by people. . . Allegedly unable to think rationally, members of less advanced societies were controlled by nature; thinking rationally, members of advanced societies controlled nature.

During the nineteenth century, the pageant of technological advancements enshrined in the Stone, Bronze, and Iron Ages made clear to intellectuals of the time that Europeans had passed through earlier stages in their progress to modernity. Anthropology developed as part of late-nineteenth-century efforts to reconstruct these past stages. . . Different peoples represented different stages in humanity's march to perfection. . . European society was the standard against which all other societies were judged."

If farming offered a better life than foraging, it would be hard to explain why many hunter-gatherer societies chose to keep eating wild food after encountering farming cultures. Indigenous hunter-gatherers in southern California traded with indigenous farmers in Arizona for two thousand years and remained hunter-gatherers anyway. In Sweden, hunter-gatherers tried farming Asian crops in 3000 BC but gave it up and went back to hunting and gathering three hundred years later. They remained hunter-gatherers for four hundred more years. Farming and foraging are more accurately viewed as different adaptive strategies that suit different geographies. Farming can offer a relatively dependable source of food in places with plentiful rainfall, a long growing season, and rich soil, but yields fluctuate in regions with harsh or unpredictable weather. Someone who lives in the tundra would have an easier time hunting marine mammals, fishing, and foraging seaweed. There's more than one way to eat.

⸘

I scraped the seeds onto the bottom of the pan with a wooden spatula. It made a clanging sound. Margot ran a honey jar under hot water to loosen the lid.

"You're an imaginative person," I said to her as we got the food ready. "What do you think would be a way to make this a more ideal city for a forager?"

She hesitated for a moment, thinking. "A lot of those areas in lower-income neighborhoods have open lots until developers come along and build houses so close together that people can spit in each other's windows," she said.

"Ah, so leaving more open space? Yeah, I agree with that," I said.

I dipped a teaspoon in the honey and drizzled it onto the toasted seeds, then added a sprinkle of sea salt. There was such a small quantity of the resulting paste that we didn't bother with utensils. We dabbed our fingers directly into the hot pan.

"It's got a nutty flavor," I said.

"If you had to eat a war god, he should taste like this," Margot said. "Yum."

12

Roundup

I came home one afternoon to find a troubling sight. Men with plastic backpacks were spraying chemicals all over the courtyard of my apartment complex. They drenched the dirt beneath the Ponderosa pine from which I pluck needles to make vitamin C tea. They soaked the grass right next to the rose bush I eat fruit from in the fall. They even went around the side of the building and sprayed the grass right up to the footpath of the alleyway where I get blackberries.

"What are you doing?" I asked.

With shrugs and broken English, one guy managed to convey to me that they were spraying Roundup because the landlord wanted it that way. "Otherwise, weeds," he said, pointing to the dirt.

"But weeds are good," I said. "Weeds are food. Weeds are medicine."

He just smiled politely and kept spraying.

I don't know if he understood what I said or not. If he did, he might have thought I was crazy. I forget how unusual

I am in embracing plants that grow without explicit human permission. It's also possible that he was ignoring me. After all, I had no authority in the situation. I was just a lowly tenant paying for the right to live in my landlord's fiefdom, and these guys were her hired hands. As I watched them spray, I wondered what, exactly, Roundup is, and if that chemical cocktail might already have gotten into something I ate, and if it had, what it might have done to my body. I wondered if it would hurt the neighbor kids who lie out on the grass in the summer, or my dog, who sets her bare paws on it daily.

Roundup is the most widely used brand of herbicide on the planet. Farmers spray it on their fields to kill plants that compete with crops. Homeowners use it to keep their lawns looking tidy. Government agencies use it on railways, highway roadsides, and utility rights-of-way. Roundup is even used in the drug war in Colombia, where the United States has spent hundreds of millions of dollars to drench coca fields by helicopter.

Roundup is formulated, packaged, and sold in America exclusively by The Scotts Miracle-Gro Company, and its active ingredient, glyphosate, is made by Monsanto. On its website, Monsanto has good things to say about glyphosate: "Conservation groups have chosen glyphosate formulations because of their effectiveness against most weeds and the fact that glyphosate has very low toxicity to wildlife. Because of its multiple uses, glyphosate has been the subject of hundreds of health, safety, and environmental studies. Regulatory agencies around the world have concluded that glyphosate herbicides pose no unreasonable risks to human health when used according to label directions."

That sounds reassuring, but when I dug deeper and read reports by environmental groups, I learned that not everyone agrees with Monsanto's conclusions. The European Union lists glyphosate as "dangerous for the environment" and "toxic for aquatic organisms." In 2011 a panel of internationally recognized experts reviewed existing studies on Roundup, including studies funded by Monsanto, and published a report analyzing them called, "Roundup and birth defects: Is the public being kept in the dark?" The report was funded by the nonprofit organization Earth Open Source, based in the United Kingdom. "Roundup and glyphosate cause endocrine disruption, damage to DNA, reproductive and developmental toxicity, neurotoxicity, and cancer, as well as birth defects. Many of these effects are found at very low doses, comparable to pesticide residues found in food and the environment," the scientists wrote.

In a section titled "Recommendations to the public," they advised: "Until the pesticide assessment process is fundamentally reformed, we recommend to the public that they do not rely on the messages of governments or industry about pesticide safety. Instead, they should take measures to protect themselves against the harmful effects of Roundup/glyphosate and other pesticides." Their suggested measures include asking supermarkets not to sell the product and lobbying local authorities.

Monsanto responded to the Earth Open Source report on its company blog, criticizing the scientists for reinterpreting a "selected set" of old data while ignoring a larger group of studies that support the company's claims to its relative safety. Monsanto's web scribes added, "To understand the herbicide's active ingredient, it helps to know that glyphosate inhibits an enzyme that is essential to plant growth; this enzyme is not found in humans or other animals, contributing to the low risk to human health from the use of glyphosate according to label directions."

That is helpful to know, but there's a big loophole here: Glyphosate is only one of the ingredients in Roundup. Roundup, like other herbicides on the market, has multiple ingredients. The other ones, the so-called inactive ingredients, are the chemicals that preserve the herbicide, make it disperse when sprayed, or adhere to and penetrate the plants. These can make up as much as 99 percent of a product, but the Environmental Protection Agency does not regulate them nor require manufacturers to list them because they are considered trade secrets. Environmental and public health groups are concerned about them because we don't know what we are being exposed to. Even The Scotts Miracle-Gro Company, which formulates those mixtures, said in a public document in 2007, "We cannot assure you that our products, particularly pesticide products, will not cause injury to the environment or to people under all circumstances."

Monsanto has a blemished record when it comes to honesty. In the 1990s, the company claimed that Roundup was "biodegradable," "practically nontoxic," and safer to eat "than table salt" until it got sued for fraud and false advertising by the attorney general of New York state and lost. This wasn't the only time Monsanto was accused of deception. In two instances, the Environmental Protection Agency caught labs hired by Monsanto falsifying data on Roundup to make it sound safer than it is.

I wasn't terribly surprised, then, when I came upon an article in *The Washington Post* with the headline "Monsanto Hid Decades of Pollution." Before Monsanto made glyphosate, it made chemicals known as PCBs, or polychlorinated biphenyls. PCBs were manufactured in the United States from 1929 to 1979, and they were used in an array of industrial products from paint to plastic. The government banned their manufacture because of their detrimental health effects, as PCBs have been shown to cause cancer and mess with motor skills, memory, the immune system, and the endocrine system. Unfortunately, PCBs are not biodegradable, so they remain in circulation around the globe, wafting through the air and water today,[31] and sometimes accumulating in the leaves and other aboveground parts of plants and food crops. The *Post's* Michael Grunwald reported that Monsanto knew about the dangers of PCBs and hid them anyway. They knew in a very graphic way—Grunwald reports they saw fish exposed to PCBs turn "belly-up within ten seconds, spurting blood and shedding skin as if dunked into boiling water," and that similarly, when the company's own study found that PCBs caused tumors in rats, they ordered

31. Residual PCBs have been implicated in cases of hermaphroditism in polar bears.

its conclusion changed from "slightly tumorigenic" to "does not appear to be carcinogenic."

"What the public is asked to accept as 'safe' today may turn out tomorrow to be extremely dangerous," Rachel Carson once wrote. [32]

⁊

If I wished for a citywide ban on lawn chemicals, I had to start close to home. I contacted my landlord via her property-management company and asked them not to spray the lawn anymore. I sent them the Earth Open Source study. I explained the benefits of a wild yard. I even pointed out that the regular mowing they're already doing will keep things looking tidy. They thanked me for my input and for "bringing this matter to [our] attention," but they kept sending out the men with backpacks and the hoses. When I pressed them to reconsider, they dismissed me. "At this time, we will not be making changes to the current lawn maintenance," they said in an e-mail.

Even though consumers have grown to distrust chemicals, preferring organic produce, 100 percent cotton t-shirts, and personal care products that boast "real" ingredients, more people use lawn chemicals[33] than ever. Ironically, environ-

32. Carson's book *Silent Spring* launched the environmental movement in the 1960s and exposed the dangers of the pesticide DDT. In it, she said, "The 'control of nature' is a phrase conceived in arrogance."

33. The overall use of agricultural pesticides has been declining since the 1970s.

mentally conscious people make up one of the fastest-growing segments of market for these chemicals. It's a seemingly incongruous trend at a time when "sustainability" is a buzzword.

My very own parents can be seen as part of this phenomenon. They care about the planet. They recycle religiously. They inspired my love of nature from a young age, enrolling me in kids' programs at the Great Swamp National Wildlife Refuge, taking me to catch frogs and listen to owls, and even sending me away to a summer camp that took me backpacking in the Appalachians. Now that I'm grown up, they read my blog. And yet they still spray their suburban lawn.

When I visited my mom and dad one recent summer, I showed them that they had two edible species growing in abundance in their backyard: the tart, lemon-flavored sorrel, *Oxalis* sp.—which looks like clover greens except the three-part leaves are heart-shaped with a crease down the center—and the mustard green bittercress, *Cardamine oligosperma*. Both are really tasty in salads. My mom and dad love salads. They eat big ones every night for dinner.

Doesn't matter. They won't budge.

"Dad, I don't understand why you insist on paying someone to spray this stuff. It's food," I said. "And judging by these weeds I see, it doesn't even work."

"We live in a nice community and we want to have our lawns look good," he said. "Our neighbors would not appreciate it if we let our lawn go wild. It would hurt their property values."

These are the same kinds of answers people gave Paul Robbins and Julie Sharp, who studied why environmentally conscious people spray their lawns. What they found is that people tend to view the lawn as public land that they're stewarding for the community in a visual sense, and so they feel an obligation to conform to local standards out of respect for their neighbors. Sometimes, the peer pressure can be intense: In the subdivision where my parents live, one dastardly resident actually engages in public shaming, sending out mass letters naming addresses of the yards he deems subpar.

The American lawn is a kind of status symbol and class marker, and that's why we see ads for herbicides with photos of vibrant green grass saying things like, "Not only will your grass be this color, your neighbors will be too." The fewer the weeds, the wealthier a homeowner appears, because it suggests she has either the leisure time to pull unwanted plants or the money to hire somebody else to do it.

This association of weeds with a lower economic class goes back at least to the late nineteenth century, when urban elites viewed manicured landscapes as expressions of affluence, order, and mankind's rightful domination over nature, and associated weeds, on the other hand, with unruliness, filth, and poverty. Authorities in Washington DC claimed that weeds gave cover to criminals waiting to attack innocent passersby. In St. Louis, politicians outlawed weeds on the absurd grounds that they polluted the air and endangered public health. The *St. Louis Post-Dispatch* actually wrote that "disease-spreading" weeds were responsible for infecting schoolchildren with typhoid, scarlet fever, and diphtheria. Residents were required to cut down any plant taller than one foot if a human had not planted it. An attorney named Smith P. Galt challenged that law in 1903 when he refused to cut down his sunflowers. His case went all the way to the Missouri Supreme Court. "Weeds are not a nuisance," Galt told the judge. Instead, he argued, they are "uncultivated vegetation" essential to the "economy of nature" and "the preservation of man upon the earth." Galt lost and was convicted of a misdemeanor.

The plants most people consider weeds today tend to be Darwin's winners. They reproduce prolifically, are particularly well suited to disturbed habitats, and are highly adaptable. Scientists dub this latter feature "phenotypic plasticity," and it means that plants can actually perceive their environment and alter their physiology in response. The dandelion lookalike known as cat's-ear, *Hypochaerus radicata*,[34] can send its leaves and stems several feet high but, as John Kallas writes in his book *Edible Wild Plants*, it has been observed to voluntarily stunt its growth and spread its leaves flat across the ground to stay below blade level when its habitat is regularly mowed. Even the flower stalks get shorter and shorter.

⅗

Lawn chemicals offer a way to project that prosperous image fairly cheaply and quickly. The EPA estimates that some forty-one million households spray herbicides. When they do, they spray a lot: Homeowners apply on average ten times more

---

34. Cat's-ear is edible. It looks just like dandelion except that it has hairy leaves and multiple blossoms branching off a single stem, whereas dandelion leaves are smooth with just one flower per stem.

pesticides[35] per acre on their lawns than farmers do in their crop fields.

Homeowners and farmers aren't the only ones pumping chemicals into the ecosystem. Timber companies are known to conduct aerial spraying on woodlands, which drift in the wind and water and expose the public to toxic chemicals the Oregon Supreme Court called "ultra-hazardous." And government officials routinely spray herbicides in wilderness areas under their control.

Ecologically speaking, the consequences are serious: When the rain touches these chemicals, the water-soluble ones flow into the sewers and sink into groundwater. All of the major rivers and streams in America are contaminated, and in a study of schoolchildren in one US city, 99 percent were found to have lawn chemicals in their bodies. One of the top-selling lawn chemicals, 2,4-D, is toxic to fish and linked to cancer in dogs. The federal NOAA Fisheries Service blames common chemicals found in more than a hundred products for threatening half of the West Coast salmon species on the endangered species list.[36]

※

The mullein I saw in a wilderness area outside the city looked healthy. It seemed like a score to find it there rather than in

35. The term "pesticide" technically denotes both herbicides and insecticides.

36. The chemicals include oryzalin, pendimethalin, and trifluralin.

one of its common urban habitats like roadsides. The fuzzy, pale green leaves were robust, and I wanted to harvest it to have on hand as lung medicine.[37] That was, until I noticed the blue dye on the ground surrounding it along with decaying Himalayan blackberry. At first I wondered what I was looking at, and then I remembered: Around here, park managers put blue dye in the herbicides. An official working for Metro, a regional governmental organization that manages fourteen thousand acres in the Portland area, told me they spray a generic version of Roundup on Himalayan blackberry, garlic mustard, hawthorn, and knotweed, all of which are edible wild plants.

"It's amazing how extensive the indoctrination has been: 'Nonnative species are bad—we've got to get rid of them,'" Mark A. Davis, author of *Invasion Biology* and chairman of the biology department at Macalester College in St. Paul, Minnesota, said in an interview with *Yale Environment 360*. "Boy, if you want nature to stop, you're going to be miserable."

When you ask officials why they spray, they invariably tell you it's because they are trying to protect and restore native ecosystems by taking out foreign plants they term "invasive species." Legally speaking, an invasive species is

37. When it comes to mullein, *Verbascum thapsus,* the word "useful" is an understatement. That weed is like the Swiss army knife of wild plants: Its stalk can be used as a spindle to make fire by friction, its roots can be pounded and used as soap or tossed into still water as fish poison, its flowers are traditionally infused into oil and used as a remedy for ear infections, and its leaves can be dried and smoked or brewed as tea for lung medicine.

a nonnative plant that's causing harm to the ecosystem it has moved into by, for example, out-competing the other plants and threatening biodiversity. In practice, the term is commonly applied much more broadly to mean any foreign species that is prolific. Many nonnative plants are mistakenly termed "harmful" when they actually improve the soil they grow in and enhance the ecosystems they move into, creating habitat for animals and full-on new niches for themselves. Some scientists wonder if intolerance toward nonnative species actually reflects a kind of xenophobia.

As the late Stephen Jay Gould wrote in 1998, the debate over invasive species "encompasses a remarkable mixture of sound biology, invalid ideas, false extensions, ethical implications, and political usages."

Even the idea of a "native plant" is tricky, because ecosystems are dynamic, not static. Like people and animals, plants have always been migrating around the world and always will, so what is native to any given place shifts based on what time period you want to think about.

Similarly, the plants we think of today as "invasive species" won't always be. Given enough time, evolution will take its course and pathogens and predators will adapt to exploit them. As apex predators, we could help that process along.

Perhaps the most loathed so-called invasive species in America is the kudzu vine, *Pueraria lobata,* a plant from Asia that took over much of the southern United States, where it is now listed as "noxious." As a forager, I can't help but think of kudzu's potential as a useful resource. Kudzu vines are said to make excellent weavers for basketry. In Traditional

Chinese Medicine, kudzu is used to treat alcoholism as well as vertigo and tinnitus. Its flowers can be made into jelly. People in Vietnam and China make food from its starchy roots. Why spray it when we can use it? I wonder the same thing when I see blackberry brambles around Portland. Blackberries are tasty, and their leaves and roots are useful as medicinal tea.[38]

Fortunately, I'm not unique in thinking this way: From the Northwest Center for Alternatives to Pesticides to the Fearless Fund in Washington DC, I have company. "There is a growing grassroots backlash against the eradication efforts of many nonnative species because of the negative effects of the chemicals and the fact that the nonnative species aren't causing the problems people accuse them of," Mark A. Davis told me. "The number of people and organizations that are becoming increasingly critical of the common eradication approach to nonnative species is definitely growing."

Even groups that do spray are beginning to recognize alternatives. Just the other day, I got an e-mail from Melissa Almendinger, executive director of the New Jersey Invasive Species Strike Team, inviting me to their second annual Invasive Species and Wild Food Potluck in Hillsborough, New Jersey. The flier encouraged attendees to bring garlic mustard pesto, grilled Japanese knotweed, or autumn olive pie.

Only a dozen kinds of plants make up eighty percent of what farmers grow, and yet there are thousands of edible

38. Blackberry leaves and roots are astringents that keep the body from losing water and work powerfully against diarrhea, which could save lives by preventing dehydration in severe cases of dysentery.

wild species in the world. Imagine how many foods we've never tasted, how many flavor combinations and textures we may never know. If we stopped spraying and started looking at unwanted plants as food, we could change the world one bite at a time.

જ

When I was visiting my parents, I went with them to see my ninety-year-old grandfather in Queens, New York. My dad and I sat outside on the front stoop next to a cherry tree. On the sidewalk ahead of us I noticed the flat black seedpod of a honey locust tree, *Gleditsia triacanthos*. I picked it up and split the hard casing open with my fingers to get at the sweet gooey pulp inside. It's golden in color and tastes like the center of a fig cookie—essentially wild candy. I passed the pod to my dad so he could have some, but he declined.

"Blech," he said, wincing. "When I was a kid, kids used to eat that stuff and get sick from the seeds, like stomachaches and stuff."

"I'm not eating the seeds, Dad. I'm eating this other stuff. It's sweet, like honey. Try it," I said.

Reluctantly, he took a piece of the pulp and tasted it.

"Not bad, huh?" I said.

"All I know is it would fall from the tree, and when I would open the pod, it would smell funny. I remember my mother saying, 'Don't eat that.' It made an impression on me. A lot of parents didn't know what it was and all they knew was some stuff could hurt you, and they didn't know which."

"Understandable. But did you like it this time?"

"I can't shake the memory of how when I was a kid, I was told they weren't good to eat," he said.

The Lerners are not exactly a foraging people. I come from a long line of city dwellers. My mom and dad were both born and raised in New York City. Both sets of their parents were born and raised in the New York metro area, too. And though my dad has traced our lineage back six generations to Romania and Poland, he hasn't even found farmer relatives.

Some people just aren't interested in foraging. I get that. So I tried a different tack in the argument. Why not at least leave the backyard alone for the other animals living out there? Why spray chemicals when you can provide food, shelter, and bedding for the nonhumans who share this planet with us instead?

"You like animals, don't you, Dad?"

"I like wildlife," he said.

"The animals eat weeds. What about them?" I asked.

"I don't know that I like them as neighbors. There's a lot here that unfortunately get hit by cars. They're overpopulated. I don't think I should feed the deer," he said.

"Now what about rabbits? They eat dandelions."

"But the rabbits also eat the flowers we plant. I think they're cute when they're little babies, but I'm not a big rabbit fan."

"Well, where do you think they're supposed to go?" I asked.

"I don't worry about it. I figure I've got other things to worry about. I see them more as a pest than as something that is helpful."

"Well, thanks for explaining your ideas," I said.

"I have a story for you," he said. "The other day Mom and I were sitting and having dinner and she saw something in the back of the yard and she called my attention to it, and I saw a red fox. It had a nice beautiful color and a fluffy tail. I liked it."

This seemed promising. "Okay, if the foxes ate weeds, would you let the lawn go wild then?"

"I'd stay out of it," my dad replied. "I'm not too involved in helping the fox or hurting the fox."

13
Slingshot

I was walking with Petunia a few streets from home when I saw an ornamental plant I wanted to eat. It was the succulent hens and chicks, *Sempervivum* sp., and it was growing out of someone's rock wall along a front yard. I had an opportunity to ask permission, because the homeowner was right there, a grown man relaxing in an inflatable kiddie pool.

"Is it okay if I eat this?" I asked.

"Oh sure. Hey, you're that girl that takes people on edible plant walks around here, right?" he said, bringing a hard lemonade to his lips. His lawn was unruly and wild, mostly filled with the dandelion lookalike cat's-ear. It was a sight I was happy to see.

"Yes, that's me," I said. "I'm so glad you don't spray your yard."

"I don't think our neighbors feel the same way, but I don't really care," he said.

"Your yard could be a little nature experiment," I said. "These weeds are only the pioneers in your landscape. Who knows what would come next. You could have a jungle right here."

I was thinking of Thoreau's essay on succession, in which he explains how wind and animals carry seeds to new habitats and species change over time. Pioneer plants are the first ones to arrive in disturbed habitats like lawns, and then, in the shade they provide, other ones come in, until eventually you may have a forest. Because urban green spaces are filled with ornamental plants from foreign regions as well as common domesticated crops and native plants, there would be no way to predict what seeds might sprout up in this yard.

As skateboarders and bicyclists coasted past, I imagined what would happen if I could somehow blink my eyes and turn this neighborhood into a forager's paradise. The lawns would be wild, fruit and nut trees would grow big and tall, and entire blocks would be left open to berry bushes and weeds. Foragers would have plenty of vegetation to choose from, and other animals would, too. Parts of it could be an old-growth forest someday.

If this vision were realized, my neighbors would benefit in myriad ways. The air would be cleaner and more breathable,[39] and the noise outside would be quieter. My neighbors' real estate values would rise: A study in Portland found that the presence of street trees added $8,870 to the sale price of a home and reduced its time on the market by about two days. Everyone would be safer because crime rates

39. In Minneapolis, a study found that urban trees remove 384 tons of air pollution per year, a service valued at $1.9 million, and that they sequester nearly nine thousand tons of carbon annually.

plummet when vegetation increases. The denser the foliage, the less property and violent crime there is. If urban foragers went around collecting fruit, nuts, and leaves in plain sight, people would feel a sense of safety as well; the effect is similar to how a neighborhood watch program inspires a sense that one's neighbors are looking out, and deters thieves. Studies show that nature is a mood-elevator with no side effects, and that it even helps to lessen physical pain. Being in nature helps people recover more quickly from ailments and injuries, too. My neighbors' quality of life would improve, and the overall health of the community would, too. When you read the studies that demonstrate these findings, you can get the impression that nature is conspiring to help us.

⚶

Plants are scientifically proven to make us feel good. The more greenery we have in our lives, the better off we are. We know this, somewhere deep inside ourselves, and we can recognize it in our attraction to all things natural. Advertisers understand it well: It's why the labels on shampoo bottles boast of "real" ingredients. It's why supermarkets put the produce at the entrance of their stores. It's why commercials for antidepressants are set in glowing, sun-lit fields. They know we're seeking nature, so they sell us its image.

We deserve more than that, and we can have it.

It is in our interest to embrace nature, to welcome the wild back into our towns and cities, and to make space for the first ways in modern life. We live in a time of great ecological crisis, a time when our need to honor the wisdom of ages past is greater than ever. In our society most people think prosperity comes from money. They think that without money there is no food. But there is food without money. There is medicine without money. Wild land is not empty; weeds are wilderness, and the wilderness is a kind of wealth. And there is wilderness in the city.

Our society is like a slingshot that's been stretched to its limits. Wilderness schools and herbal medicine programs are proliferating, and foraging is on the rise. We're setting ourselves free now, soaring back to nature.

14

The Way of the Raccoon

For years before it came to mean eating plants, the phrase "urban foraging" meant collecting food from the garbage. Though Google knows better, Wikipedia still thinks that's the only definition. When I read that entry, I thought of my old friend Adam Weissman, an avid Dumpster diver and activist in New York City who became the freegan movement's de facto spokesperson after writing a manifesto online. Freegans—the term is an amalgamation of "vegan" and "free"—seek to live without money. Just as vegans boycott meat products, freegans boycott The System. They squat in foreclosed homes or barter services in exchange for free rooms, sew their own clothes out of scrap fabric, and ride bicycles instead of driving cars. Millions of people learned about freegan philosophy from Adam's quotes in the *New York Times,* or by watching him explain it on the TV show *20/20*. "Freeganism is a reaction to waste," Adam told Britain's *The Independent* newspaper, "but also to the injustices like sweatshops and the destruction of the rain forests that go into producing goods in the first place. I realized that, as a purchasing consumer, I was complicit in that exploitation. But by consuming waste, I'm not supporting these practices." Adam has since renounced freeganism as a philosophy, even though he still Dumpster dives most of his food. He thinks it's useful to get free stuff but that, as a political critique, it's hollow because it doesn't change anything.

A lot of people Dumpster dive. My friend Brent is one of them. He is a tall, lanky guy with blonde dreads. I haven't heard him go off on The Man, but he lives the lifestyle: He's rarely employed, hardly ever pays rent, and yet always has a comfortable place to sleep and plenty of food to share. So when he offered to take me on a tour of the city's best trash bins, I thought, *Why not learn the way of the raccoon?*

I drove up to the house where he was staying and watched impatiently as he took a long time saying farewell to a bunch of granola-looking women on the front porch. Finally—finally—he walked down the stairs. My annoyance melted when I noticed that he was carrying handfuls of flowers. "For you," he said, arranging white roses and purple clover blossoms to dry on my dashboard. Knowing Brent, the roses were almost certainly clipped from neighboring yards, but I dismissed the thought, because a stolen rose smells just as sweet as a purchased one.

We had decided to take my car instead of riding our bicycles because it would be easier to cover large distances across the city and haul back big quantities to his friends' place that way—he was staying with eight roommates—but also because the idea of riding down busy streets at night in traffic with just a helmet and a prayer for protection freaked me out. I'd read in a local newspaper that a 2010 study by Oregon Health and Sciences University found that 20 percent of Portland bicyclists had endured a "traumatic event" while commuting in the past year. I'm waiting for the invention of bike-only corridors, which I thought existed only in my imagination, until I heard it's all the rage in Europe. New York City has the right idea, too, with its new bike lanes that are separated from cars by planters.

Our first stop on the Trash Cans of Portland VIP Tour was a free dinner in Colonel Summers Park in southeast Portland put on by Food Not Bombs, a grassroots network of activists who provide hot vegetarian meals in public outdoor spaces. The food is usually either donated by area grocery stores or scavenged. I was curious to see who came to eat, as I had heard it described as a social event for activists. I followed Brent to a grassy field next to a playground where a dozen people sat on the ground, eating and talking. One or two were older men who looked like they might be homeless, but the rest appeared to be average Portlanders in their twenties dressed in grunge punk attire. Brent handed me an old yogurt container to use as a bowl and said hello to a few people he recognized, including two young women who carefully ladled out big cupfuls of watery vegetable soup for us, and a thin, bearded, weathered-looking man in his forties who was wearing a Jesus-style garment and introduced himself as Satya. In Sanskrit "satya" means truth. Brent told me later that he was a preacher of sorts, inspired by Hindu priests he had heard about who live off the generosity of others.

As we ate, we heard a small circle of Native American men beating animal skin drums nearby. As the beats thumped, I realized that although this concept of free dinner by and for the community felt unfamiliar and radical, because it was happening without an exchange of money, it was actually the way of life on this land for much longer than it wasn't. The modern way is really the strange one.

We hopped back in the car and headed to a small, independent, high-end grocery store in a trendy neighborhood. Brent lifted the lid on a green compost bin and pulled out four bouquets of orange tiger lilies and purple, white, and rose-colored carnations. Next came an assortment of bruised produce: two zucchini, a bunch of red seedless grapes, several ears of corn, two avocados, and a handful of potatoes and apples. Out of everything, I was most excited about the flowers. Flowers, a farmer once told me, are what happens when nature smiles.

Next we headed to a pasta factory. We saw four plastic garbage cans against a metal garage door, and we heard chains creaking and clanging against the concrete floor inside. It seemed the door might open at any moment, and I was concerned we'd get in trouble for trespassing. Brent lifted a lid, reached an arm inside, and pulled up giant handfuls of ravioli, covering himself in flour in the process. He said he was sure it had been made earlier that day because the same bins were empty when he had looked in them for food the night before. Beneath the ravioli, which was stuffed with smoked salmon, there were gobs and gobs of sliced white cheese stuck together. He tasted it and exclaimed, "Parmesan!" We worked quickly to load the pasta and cheese into milk crates and lugged what ended up being fifty pounds worth of food into the trunk of my car. It was an amazing abundance, and we couldn't wait to share it. As I tried to imagine how much it would cost to buy this quantity of fresh, handmade food, I started to feel an endorphin high that only increased when I saw the offerings at the next stop: a "free porch"—a local residence known for giving away donated food to the community on a weekly basis.

There were boxes and boxes of just-expired organic juices on the sidewalk, carrot-beet concoctions, and leafy greens, the kind that go for $8 a jug at the fancy grocery stores. On the porch we saw paper bags filled with loaves of different kinds of bread, some of which was hard, but all of which was edible.[40] It was an impressive bounty. Brent and I carried big clumps of ravioli and Parmesan in our arms and urged everyone we saw to take it home with them.

It was at that moment that I truly felt wealthy. In fact, I felt the richest I have ever felt in my life. My car was stuffed with food and flowers. I felt like I'd won the lottery. I thought of the Indian philosopher Osho, who wrote, "If you want to be rich, be generous." I thought of how I would revise that to say, "If you want to feel rich, be generous." I thought of another Osho writing, too: "When you share, you thank him that he allowed you to pour your energy—which was getting too much upon you, it was getting heavy. You feel grateful.

40. Hardened bread could be heated to soften or toasted. Bruschetta, anyone?

Sharing is out of your abundance. Charity is for others' poverty. Sharing is out of your richness. There is a qualitative difference." I know what he meant.

That degree of abundance had never really happened to me while foraging plants. When I harvest plants, I feel keenly aware that I am impacting an ecosystem—stinging nettle may be hosting butterfly larvae, for instance—and, especially in an urban setting, there is almost always a sense of scarcity, of limited space, a feeling that there's not enough to go around and I need to be conservative in my picking. With Dumpster diving, though, you're indulging in what someone else has already consented to give away and toss in a heap. You're reveling in the riches without stepping on anyone's toes. It feels very positive. When you find gobs of gourmet pasta, is there any other thought besides, "Let's call everyone we know and have a great feast"?

No doubt some will say, "That's great and all, but if it's thrown away, is it really fit to eat?" Sometimes it isn't. I got a little caught up in the excitement of the score and ate some things without cooking or even rinsing them, like grapes and ravioli. I probably should not have done that, because the next morning I shit blood. Not to worry—I drank some Oregon grape tincture and felt fine by the next day.

Increasingly, the phrase "urban foraging" has come to denote what I do, which is harvesting wild plants in a city.[41]

41. "I will arm-wrestle you over the phrase 'urban foraging,' but you've always been in better shape than me, so I'll lose," Adam said to me on Facebook the other day.

There is little data on how many people forage today,[42] but we do know that the past decade has seen a resurgence of plant harvesting in cities, most visibly among coordinated groups dedicated to collecting fruit and nuts in public spaces, such as Fallen Fruit in Los Angeles and the Portland Fruit Tree Project in Oregon, and also among individuals. In New Zealand, Maori people harvest up to fifty-eight kinds of plants in urban public areas and roadsides. In Seattle, local foragers told anthropologists that they collect 433 different plant species, including bark, cones, buds, flowers, sap, leaves, fruit, seeds, pollen, branches, stems, shoots, roots, and tubers. This kind of urban foraging is a relatively new phenomenon as a cultural trend, although plant foraging itself, of course, is not.

If urban foraging as I do it is a semantic relative of Dumpster diving, so is urban gleaning. Gleaners have historically collected the remnants of produce in post-harvest farm fields. In

42. Eighteen percent of people surveyed by phone randomly in New England told researchers they had foraged in the past year, and that figure may be applicable to the broader continent. Around the world, many people forage to supplement their diet. In America, some are immigrants from Russia or Italy collecting mushrooms in the forest, others are people of Asian descent gathering ferns along the coast, and still others are rural folks picking wild huckleberries and living off the land. Few cultures forage full time anymore. Hunter-gatherer tribes today "often live on cultural 'frontiers,' shifting between foraging and wage labor or commercial foraging. . . . For others, foraging is a political message, a way to reaffirm their cultural worth," Robert L. Kelly writes. "Due to the ubiquity of trade, there can be little doubt that all ethnographically known hunter-gatherers are tied into the world economic system in one way or another; in some cases they have been so connected for hundreds of years," he says. "The Penan of Borneo gather rattan today for the world market and probably traded with Chinese merchants at least as long ago as 900 AD."

cities, they collect fallen fruit on residential streets and donate it to local soup kitchens and to neighbors. Gleaners tend to collectively plan and orchestrate their haul within a community, whereas Dumpster diving and plant foraging are typically more individual, spontaneous pursuits. There are differences in jargon, too. Urban gleaners describe what they do as "redistributing waste" and "cleaning up" the clutter on the street. While the intention behind this sort of thing is obviously good-hearted, the language is problematic: It objectifies plants and implies that they have worth only insofar as they feed human mouths or comply with our aesthetic preferences. But plants are inherently valuable living creatures, part of the urban eco-system, and they invariably support an interconnected web of myriad animals—human and not—who live here.

Human foragers are a diverse crowd. We come from all ethnicities and live in all parts of the country. We are all ages and span all income brackets and have an array of political views and religions. And yet, surveys have found some con-sistencies among us. One is that we often list spirituality as a motivator, perhaps because foraging is a primal behavior that ties us to something deep and expansive within ourselves. Another is that few foragers harvest food plants commercially or sell what we gather. When foragers do give away wild food we have harvested with our own hands, we often do so in the form of a gift or barter. There seems to be an inclination to view foraged goods as existing outside the space of commerce, law, and other civilized institutions—a feeling that the wild is sacred.

PART FOUR:

I Think I Love You

15

Plant People

At the end of an urban nature walk I led last spring, my class came to a small neighborhood park with maple and sycamore trees. I asked everyone to sit down and relax on the grass, and then I invited them to take part in an open-ended experiment. It begins when I pass around a tincture bottle with a plant extract I've made. It's always something very gentle and safe to consume, such as wild carrot or elderberry, and I always know what it is, but it has no label on it, and I keep its identity secret from everyone else.

"If you read up on ethnobotany, the study of plant use across different cultures, you find that indigenous people all over the world use similar strategies in how they go about learning plant medicine. Certainly they pass down stories from generation to generation, and observe animals, and there is some trial and error, but they also say they learn things from the plants themselves directly, that they receive messages through dreams or in meditation," I tell the class. "I don't know what the mechanism of action might possibly be, but I do know that if all these cultures all over the world are all having the same experience, then it is at least possible that it's a real phenomenon, and if it is a real phenomenon, then maybe it will work for us, too."

There's a line I like in the book *Autobiography of a Yogi* by Paramhansa Yogananda: "The only scientific attitude one can take on any subject is whether it is true. The law of gravitation worked as efficiently before Newton as after him."

ॐ

I ask people to put a few drops of the tincture on their tongues and then sit quietly and meditate for a few minutes to see what happens next, after which time everyone shares their experience with the group.

"You may feel hot or cold, tired or energized, or you may find your awareness moving to a certain part of your body," I tell them. "Pay attention to anything that happens for you. It is all potentially meaningful."

The methodology of this experiment is not my own invention. It's practiced by many herbalists who believe that plants heal us in spiritual as well as physical ways, and who embrace an animistic perspective of the world. In Portland, the School of Forest Medicine, run by Scott Kloos, is a nexus of this approach. "This is the way people have learned about plants forever," Scott told me.

"To my mind the important thing is not appropriating the wisdom or ritual of other cultures who seem to 'get it,' but for each of us in local community groups to connect with the wisdom around us—from the spirits of the land where we live," he wrote on a blog. "The wisdom and intelligence of the universe surrounds us: we actually have to work very hard and expend a lot of energy to keep it out. It only takes a slight adjustment of perception to allow the wisdom of the universe to penetrate into our consciousness and hearts."

This idea that plants have wisdom has been explored in pop culture, particularly in terms of the exotic entheogens ayahuasca and iboga. Ayahuasca is a mixture of plant medicines native to Peru; iboga is made from the root bark of a tree that grows in west-central Africa (found in Gabon and Cameroon). Ayahuasca and iboga are both used in ceremonial rites by indigenous people of those regions, and for westerners of a less spiritual mind-set, they are very powerful "psychedelics." Ayahuasca, the more widely known of the two, is a tea brewed from a mixture of the jungle vine yagé, *Banisteriopsis caapi,* and the leaf of the chacruna plant, *Psychotria viridis,* along with other ingredients that vary.

"The vine in and of itself can be overtly psychoactive, but it is in the combination of the two that the magic happens. When I drank in the Amazon, I had the opportunity to collect various plants with a shaman that were to be added to the brew. Some were, according to him, for 'making the bones strong' or 'to make you beautiful to the spirits,'" Scott told me. "On the pharmacological level, the vine contains harmine and harmaline, which are MAO inhibitors that make the DMT in the leaf orally active. The vine represents the masculine principle and brings force and grounding; the leaf is the feminine and brings the visions and opening to the astral."

The visions do not come without a cost. Daniel Pinchbeck, one of the most famous authors on entheogens in America, wrote about drinking ayahuasca with a shaman and then purging violently out of every orifice in his book *Breaking Open the Head*. I read a similar account in *National Geographic Adventure* magazine by Kira Salak, who said that while she had to hold onto a "vomit bucket," her ayahuasca experience effectively condensed decades of therapy into several powerful nights of healing—she had epiphanies that broke through her years-long struggle with depression.

Not long after I read Kira's article, I began to see ads on the Internet for ayahuasca retreats. In exchange for airfare and several thousand dollars, anyone can fly to the Amazon to vacation with witch doctors who will preside over your ayahuasca journey. My friend Adam Elenbaas went on one such trip to a place called the Blue Morpho Lodge in Peru. He came back wiser than before, and with a great deal of insight into his childhood traumas and his difficult relationship with his father. He wrote a memoir about the transformative realizations he had—as well as the frightening entities he saw while in the ayahuasca trance—called *Fishers of Men: The Gospel of an Ayahuasca Vision Quest.*

I thought it interesting that Adam and Kira and Daniel all said they perceived ayahuasca to be an intelligent presence guiding their visions and leading them to awakenings in the spiritual realm. This lines up with the views of animistic hunter-gatherer tribes and indigenous cultures all over the world, who believe that plants—and all of nature—are sentient and conscious, and that we can communicate with them. Ayahuasca can be seen as a high-powered launch pad into that reality, and visions a state of communion.

Advocates of plant-spirit healing say that gentler approaches work, too, and that sitting in front of a tree with an open mind is enough to create the space for communication from plants without the purging and the travel expense. "We need not go to the Amazon seeking Plant Teachers," Scott writes. "We are surrounded by teachers wherever we live. Some teachers are indigenous to the land and wait for us while others, like St. John's Wort,[43] follow us around establishing themselves in the disturbed lands left in the wake of human progress. They follow us to help mend the disturbed parts of our psyches and souls so that we may return to a state of wholeness and recognize the sacredness of all that surrounds us."

Plant-spirit healing isn't just about visions. Some people just want to get information on a given plant's medicinal properties straight from the plant. Meditation with non-psychoactive tinctures, especially in a group setting, can be one such way to find out.

や

I pulled a dandelion tincture out of my bag and dropped a few squirts of the extract into my mouth. It tasted very strongly of alcohol and burned on my tongue, and I winced.

43. In herbal jargon, the word "wort" means useful herb, usually (but not always) with a medicinal connotation. A plant colloquially termed a "lung wort," for example, is an herb that acts on the lungs. Mugwort, *Artemisia vulgaris,* was once commonly used in beer brewing—clearly, it is useful for the mug.

I passed the bottle to my right, and the dozen or so people in my class that day each took a taste. We sat there quietly together for just a few minutes. I noticed traffic and the sound of some kids slapping a basketball against the pavement on a nearby court. My students were sitting very seriously with straight backs and closed eyes.

A crow interrupted us with a startling caw. "That's our cue," I said. "Let's share."

I told everyone I'd share last, so as not to taint the results of our experiment, since I knew what the tincture was made of.

Some of the students were apprehensive to say anything, perhaps worried about being wrong or saying something silly, but then an older guy was willing to break the ice.

"I'll go," he said. "I got an image of what the plant looks like. It has serrated leaves and a yellow flower, so I guess that means it's dandelion."

I was shocked. There was no way he could have known what it was.

Weirder still, he was far from the only person to nail a mystery tincture. Results were not always this impressive every time I did the experiment with a class, but people often correctly guessed the color of an herb's flower and its name, or noticed sensations in the part of the body it acts on, even if they knew nothing about the plant before that moment.

꽃

The first time I met Erico, the herbalist, was in a quiet park in southeast Portland on a beautiful autumn afternoon. We sat on a bench and watched leaves blow in the wind as squirrels chased each other around maple trees. I had invited him there because I was writing an article about herbalism for a newspaper. He didn't know anything about me other than that. He just handed me an unmarked bottle with a wry smile and encouraged me to take a taste of the tincture inside and tell him what I thought. The flavor was bitter on my tongue.

For no reason at all, I asked, "Is it a root?"

He looked surprised. "You've done this before?"

"So I'm right?" I asked.

"Yes, it's burdock root."

How did this happen?

I have no idea. But it did.

ॐ

Herbalist author Stephen Buhner suggests in *The Secret Teaching of Plants: The Intelligence of the Heart in the Direct Perception of Nature* that perhaps the mechanism for plant-human communication is the merging of the electromagnetic fields emanating from all living beings and the resulting exchange of energy through the meeting of these invisible fields. Buhner says it is the heart, and not the brain or mind, that is the bodily organ responsible for this kind of phenomenon. Others wonder if psychoactive plant medicines work by opening one's consciousness to different frequencies, as if tuning a radio dial to one of the many other dimensions physicists tell us are part of our universe. Who can say?

꙰

The very first time I participated in a plant-spirit experiment was in one of Emily's classes. We passed around the bottle, and I squeezed some pale yellow liquid out of the medicine dropper and onto my tongue. The flavor of alcohol was very strong, but the medicine also tasted slightly sweet. I closed my eyes and waited to feel something.

I didn't notice any sensations, but I had a vivid daydream that a jolly little elf-like fellow in a jester's hat came skipping across the room, placed his hands on my shoulders, and shook me, bringing an image of a fuzzy black-and-white television screen to mind, and then he skipped off. Later Emily told the group that our mystery tincture was dandelion.

When I saw dandelions in my neighborhood after that, I noticed that I perceived a subtle but playful vibe from them, in the same way I would perceive a mood or a personality in a dog or a human friend, or in the way that you walk into a room and feel instantly at ease or, conversely, totally unwelcome. I wondered if I could sense a mood or personality from other kinds of plants, and I discovered that in fact I could. Some would seem to me to be masculine and others would feel more feminine, while others still would come off gender-neutral. Douglas-fir trees feel wise and serious to me, paternal even, whereas Western red cedar trees seem graceful and maternal. I find that chickweed feels light-hearted and childlike, and that maple trees have a very gentle, supportive, youthful androgyny to them.

I cannot be sure whether I am truly perceiving something external to me or if I am just projecting, but I do think it's interesting that when I've shared my observations with friends who have tried this too, they have concurred and said they had the same impressions of the energies and personalities of plants and trees.

As Erico said to me one day, "A solipsist can't say if anyone exists at all except himself. So do we know if plants are conscious? We don't. It's a feeling that we get from them."

I make no claims that I understand how any of this happens, but it sure does happen, and in the context of many other cultures, what I am describing is so commonplace as to be mundane.

In western culture, we accept as real only that which we know how to explain, or how to measure objectively and with repetition. The difficulty in translating these results into a scientific mold is that plant-spirit communication is a set of largely subjective experiences. Science is dismissive of subjective experiences, but subjective experiences are just as real as objective ones. It's like falling in love: You know it when you're in it, even if you don't know how you got there.

The idea that plants could communicate with us is hard to swallow if we think that the only way to communicate is with a voice box and a brain. Must a person—human or otherwise—have a brain in order to be conscious? For that matter, what is consciousness? And how do we measure it? These questions are puzzling to philosophers and scientists alike.

"We have no idea how consciousness emerges from the physical activity of the brain and we do not know whether consciousness can emerge from non-biological systems, such as computers . . . At this point the reader will expect to find a careful and precise definition of consciousness. You will be disappointed. Consciousness has not yet become a scientific term that can be defined in this way. Currently we all use the term *consciousness* in many different and often ambiguous ways. Precise definitions of different aspects of consciousness will emerge . . . but to make precise definitions at this stage is premature," eight neuroscientists wrote in the book *Human Brain Function,* in 2004.

To find out if the next eight years had changed anything, in 2012 I checked in with Professor Valerie Hardcastle, editor of the *Journal of Consciousness Studies*[44] and dean of the McMicken College of Arts and Sciences at the University of Cincinnati, where she specializes in cognitive neuroscience and philosophy of mind. "There is no consensus on what consciousness is," the professor said. "Some experts believe that consciousness is tied to the brain; others believe that it is not necessarily."

She added: "On the other hand, I think most people know what you mean when you say 'consciousness.' It is

44. The *Journal of Consciousness Studies* is an interdisciplinary, peer-reviewed publication whose contributors are scholars and scientists at the top of their fields in cognitive science, philosophy, biology, neuroscience, and psychology.

kind of like jazz that way—you know what people are talking about even if you can't define it exactly."

The *Oxford English Dictionary* defines "conscious" as an adjective that means "having knowledge or awareness; able to perceive or experience something," such as "one's surroundings" or "one's sensations, thoughts, feelings, etc.," which sounds about right to me. A considerable amount of scientific study has gone into documenting plant perception, showing that plants can solve problems and adapt to environmental conditions by, for example, growing toward light; that plants can sense magnetic fields; that they respond to touch;[45] that they defend themselves against predators; that they seem to store memories and learn from their experiences; and even that they can communicate with one another.

One of the ways plants communicate is underground, sending chemical messages back and forth through the symbiotic network of fungal mycorrhizae and roots; another way is aboveground, by releasing volatile organic compounds into the air when under attack, which neighboring plants can then detect and use as a cue to steel their defenses.[46] To defend themselves, plants can turn different

45. The "sensitive plant," *Mimosa pudica,* folds its leaves when you touch it. The Venus flytrap, *Dionaea muscipula,* responds carnivorously when it feels an insect's touch.

46. Responses have been documented among lima beans, cotton, willow, tobacco, corn, and other plants. For example, blueberry shrubs, *Vaccinium corymbosum,* exposed to warning VOCs (Volatile Organic Compounds) from neighboring shrubs subsequently had 70 percent fewer gypsy moth larvae infesting them than blueberry shrubs that had not been exposed to the warning chemicals.

parts of their genetic code on or off in order to produce toxins, or change the structure of their leaves, making them tougher or less palatable to whoever may try to eat them. They can even release chemicals that attract predators to the pests that are plaguing them. Most impressive of all, some plants can actually communicate with sound, just like people do. According to an article in the journal *Trends in Plant Science* in summer 2012, the roots of young corn plants make clicking noises, which their neighbors can hear and respond to.

"Plant behaviors have been characterized as simpler than those of animals. Recent findings challenge this notion by revealing high levels of sophistication previously thought to be within the sole domain of animal behavior," scientist Richard Karban of the University of California, Davis, wrote in the journal *Ecology Letters.*

Can plants be called intelligent? Depends on whom you ask. Some scientists I talked to said yes, and others hesitated to use the term, even while agreeing that plants meet the criteria. "Yes, plants are highly adapted to the environment, but 'intelligent' seems like a goofy descriptor to me," said Professor Anurag Agrawal of the Department of Ecology and Evolutionary Biology at Cornell University. Others, such as Professor Anthony Trewavas of the Institute for Molecular Plant Science at the University of Edinburgh, have no problem using it. "Some think that only humans can be intelligent, since that [being human] is the criterion they impose on every other organism," he said. "Intelligence is merely problem solving."

Plants don't have brains that look like ours, but they do produce some of the same hormones and neurochemicals that humans do, and some experts believe that plants may have something akin to a decentralized brain and nervous system. It is possible that we are more similar than we think and just have different bodies. If we look way back in the evolutionary lineage, plants and humans do share common ancestors.

What if plants are conscious? The implications would be sweeping. Matthew Hall, author of *Plants As Persons: A Philosophical Botany,* thinks we should view plants as "other-than-human persons" who deserve to be respected, thanked, and considered. He says that vegetarians would do well to adopt the Jain ethos of minimizing harm, and that we should kill plants only out of necessity like conscientious hunters.

If plants are conscious, and nature is largely made of plants, then nature is conscious. If nature is conscious, then Earth is not merely a web of mechanically reflexive predators and prey but something much more magical than that: a vibrant, interdependent collective of living, thinking beings that extends everywhere across the planet. It's alive.

16

Horsetail

Airplanes buzzed overhead, interrupting a chorus of crickets as the quarter-moon ascended in the late August sky. I lay on my back on the sandy ground and watched the last bits of sunlight shine through a tangle of cottonwood branches. Some fiery rays pierced through and others got snared in the shadows. Earlier I had gone wandering through the park's fourteen hundred acres of meadow and woodland with Petunia. We walked through fields of flowering goldenrod, along a river dotted with stinging nettle and willow shrubs, and in the shade where red-osier dogwood and horsetail grow. We were just outside the trees now, resting off the trail next to some horsetail and Queen Anne's lace. Whenever I see horsetail, *Equisetum arvense,* I think of dinosaurs. Horsetail goes back in the fossil records as far as three hundred million years ago when dragonflies were the size of herons. Now it's only three feet tall and skinny as a pencil, but it was once forty feet high and thick as a broad tree.[47]

As I lay there, I thought of how I might have missed this beautiful sunset had it not been for foraging. The very first time I came to this park was just to give Petunia a place to run around and dig for moles, but as we explored the land, I noticed some young stinging nettle here and there, particularly in partial shade near the water. The nettle came to mind later when I went to a cafe and saw spinach quiche in the display case. I thought, "Why not make nettle quiche?" I looked up some spinach quiche recipes on the internet and discovered that it was very simple to make: All you do is sauté the greens, put them in a piecrust, and then cover it with cheese and a mixture of whisked milk and egg. It was easy enough to buy a premade piecrust, and I knew I could substitute the dairy with some nut milk and cheese alternative. When I came back to the park to harvest, I brought a backpack and a pair of scissors with me. I knew the layout of the land well enough to get us from the parking lot to the water, but I wasn't sure where the big patches would be. This presented a challenge. Wandering wasn't something I tended to do in parks before then. I don't have a good sense of direction. I worried that if I wandered then I might get lost, and if I got lost, it might be a long time before I figured out where I was. I stayed close to the trail this time, just in case. Since I didn't know in my head where to go, I decided to make a little game of it and let my

47. Horsetail still reproduces using a primitive method. Like ferns and mushrooms, it drops spores. The plant is also useful. The stalk has a sandpaper texture you can use to file down your nails or scour dishes.

Horsetail

heart lead the way, taking me into the bushes wherever it felt was right.

When I saw a little cove of cottonwood trees on a slope, I felt drawn to it. There wasn't any water nearby, which to my thinking meant it was an unlikely spot for nettle, but I went anyway. I carefully stepped over some thorny Himalayan blackberry canes and was glad I had on long sleeves and long pants as I brushed past the prickles of teasel and thistle in the way. Petunia stood back and watched me, not daring to make her way into the thorns. Just beyond them I got under the trees into the cove, and I found myself standing amidst what had to be a full acre of nettle. I could not believe how big this patch was—it's the biggest I have ever seen. I snipped the tops of just about four cups worth of plants—only as much as I knew I would use for the quiche—and transferred them into my bag using my scissors as tongs. At home I sautéed them with wild mustard greens and poured it into a piecrust, using hazelnut milk and nutritional yeast as nondairy substitutes, and it was delicious. I liked it so much that I returned to the park weekly to harvest nettle and let Petunia run around. I ate hardly any other produce the whole spring season.

Each time I came back, I liked the park more than the time before. I got to know the landscape well enough to feel comfortable trying out new trails. When the nettle got tall and flowered in early summer, I stopped harvesting it for food as much. I came back anyway, though, and pretty soon I felt brave enough to really wander. I'd run with Petunia into the tall amber grasses and crouch down so she couldn't see me and then spring up again as we played a little game of hide-and-seek. Sometimes I would notice little game trails in the grass, thin depressions flattened out by small animals like rabbits and coyotes. I got to exploring them on my hands and knees, crawling through tunnels of lupine and Queen Anne's lace all the way up to blackberry caverns that I am much too big to slip into. Other times we'd walk far in any given direction and end up at a pond, where we'd see frogs and garter snakes and tiny spider mites I took to calling Red Dot Creatures before I figured out what they were. Whenever I was thinking of going there, I'd say, "Petunia, do you want to go to Paradise?" and she'd get very excited, because she knew she was about to spend a few hours in dog heaven.

I watched two bees climb around on some goldenrod flowers during that sunset. I had brought a tape recorder with me, so that I could say exactly how I felt about the park that evening and remember it. I knew that I had something important to realize about what I was experiencing in my heart here, because I have never experienced it anywhere else.

"Even if I have no idea where exactly I am in this park, I know I am safe," I began. "It's like the land knows me. It's like a mutual recognition that just comes up inside me—this peace and happiness, this feeling that everything's going to be okay. It's better than having gone to yoga class, the sense of calm. There's actually a sense of love in it. It's an amazing thing; that's the feeling in my heart when I come here. I don't just feel love for it, I feel loved. As I say that it actually brings tears to my eye. I feel loved by this land. It's like the land remembers me and I remember it and we're both friends. There's a fondness."

Horsetail

When you care about somebody, when you're in a relationship with somebody and it gets to the point where you love each other, you desire to show your beloved the utmost kindness, and to express how much you care for him or her. It's the same way when you fall in love with land. It's a two-way relationship. If one party is using the other, it's unhealthy and controlling. It's out of balance. As a culture, we are out of balance. Conventional agriculture can be like a dominating boyfriend who forces his girlfriend to change to meet his specifications. Foraging is like a sweet one who loves her for exactly who she is.

⚭

There's a stand of sitka willow that I like to harvest on the beach of the Columbia River. It grows very close to the water, next to a whole bunch of not-yet-ripe Himalayan blackberry and bright yellow tansy flowers. It's right on the sand, and I can easily see Washington state right across the water. Sometimes sailboats are out there, depending on the season. I take gardening shears with me when I visit and clip the young branches to turn into dream catchers that I make by hand and then give away as gifts to friends and family. I save the crow feathers I find on the street in the city and hang them from leather strips I tie to the bottom of the frame. I pick the willow branches when they're only about as thick as a pencil. I bend them back on themselves while they're still on the shrub to see how pliable they are. Sometimes the bark is neon green and other times it's more of a brown-red. I like the variation. It's easy to find good ones.

I have read that dream catchers originated as an Ojibwe craft, but since then many other tribes adopted them and it has become a general American Indian art form. I am not of native descent. I don't want to steal anybody's culture so much as be inspired by it. I could see how somebody could view my making dreamcatchers as cultural appropriation, but I see these creations as artistic extensions of myself: I am often able to remember three or more dreams per night, and I see meaning in them. I have an affinity for spiders, too. I trap them in my home rather than kill them. I set aside a glass jar for this purpose. The label on it says "Arachnid Relocation Project." What I do is cover the spider with the jar and then slip a piece of paper in between the opening of the jar and the surface I've trapped it against, such as a wall. Then I hold the paper to the jar as I turn it and tap it lightly if the spider is up there, and then I screw on a lid.

श

I went to that willow spot the other day at sunset. I sank my toes into the sand as the summer breeze swept over my shoulders. I clipped four branches and pulled off the leaves while my dog ran around off leash, making friends with the people who were barbecuing nearby. She can sniff out potential table scraps from a surprising distance.

The people barbecuing didn't seem to mind. It's the kind of spot where anything goes. The beach is littered with broken beer bottles and half-smoked cigarettes and broken Styrofoam cups. Some people live in tents there and high school kids secretly drink beer there and I often see people having bonfires. There's a ton of litter blowing around. "Disrespectful," I want to whisper under my breath. But I don't, because I get why people litter—it's just instinct. Until very recently, everything was biodegradable, and it was no big deal to discard spent food like that. It could even be viewed as natural. We would throw our half-eaten fruit on the ground and watch trees spring up from the pits.

There's another reason I don't judge the litterbugs: They give me an opportunity to do something kind. Before I started foraging, I was not the kind of person who picked up other people's trash. But now I have a pantry stocked with heavy glass jars filled with golden brown tinctures. I have a stockpile of plant medicines that can effectively treat the flu, pneumonia, staph, strep throat, urinary tract infections, allergies, diabetes, fatigue, anxiety, headaches, migraines, lymphatic infections, constipation, diarrhea, and food poisoning. I have little jars of cottonwood salve, made with beeswax and olive oil, that can disinfect wounds. The room I used to think of as my office now looks much more like an apothecary, with big bunches of lemon balm and comfrey and stinging nettle hanging to dry from a string between my shelves. The shelves hold jars of chestnut flour, rose hips, dried mullein leaves, black walnuts, and hazelnuts. I am the recipient of an incredible bounty, a limitless array of gifts. I have been blessed and for no other reason than that I learned to see them.

I pick up soda cans and glass beer bottles and empty bags of marshmallows. I look at the water and the plants next to it and the big expanse of sky. "Thank you," I say.

17

Nocturne

There's nothing quite like the stillness of the city well after midnight, especially in the spring, when the moon lights the stars and the white-blossomed cherry trees are all aglow. The wind scatters perfumed petals across the sidewalk, and everyone is asleep but for me. Petunia and I like to walk at this hour because it feels like the world is a dream standing still.

I look at the dark road, and I think back to when I was driving my car on a New Jersey highway years ago, back to that moment when I first felt the disconnect, became aware of the strangeness of the buzzing techno-future in which we live and the fact that our Stone Age bodies evolved to exist in a very different world. I feel differently now. I feel more rooted on Earth now, more human. I see that I am nature—that we are all are nature, and always have been.

When I first began foraging in the city, I viewed wild plants as just-in-case disaster insurance, something meant to stay on the fringes of my life. But what I learned over the next four years is that they are much, much more than that. Not only are wild plants food and medicine, but they also offer us a way to connect with each other, to build community, and to access our deepest selves. Foraging brings with it a consciousness-shifting transformation of vision that reveals hidden treasure. It leads us far beyond the limits of dualistic frameworks like human versus nature or city versus wilderness: We find the wilderness within.

Petunia and I rounded a corner when a blur of motion caught my eye. She didn't see them, but I did. There they were: two raccoons sitting shoulder to shoulder on the sidewalk, gray fur and black bandit masks illuminated by a streetlamp spotlight. The domestic urban forager stared at the two wild ones. The two wild ones stared back at her. We held our gaze for an unlikely series of minutes in a serendipitous communion of like minds, and then they ran away.

Who doesn't love a great movie, the all-knowing oracle that is the Internet, or our ability to leap from Los Angeles to New York in hours instead of months? Modernity is not without its charms. It strikes me, though, that in our torrid embrace of technology we have forgotten that the natural world is just as magical—maybe even more. Sit in front of a tree and you are looking at the incarnation of a three-hundred-million-year-old being that eats sunlight and drinks rain. The dirt on which we walk is made of stars. Dig under the pavement and you find the bones of saber-toothed tigers.

Every wild plant is a link to what once was and to what could be. It's all here, still. We have only to remember.

Dandelion Hunter

Appendix A: Selected Wild Recipes

Note: Please check with your doctor before eating unfamiliar foods or experimenting with herbal smoke blends, especially if you have any concerns or ailments.

MARGOT BERLIN'S DANDELION SPICE COFFEE
Note: This is a three-part recipe.

Part One: Roast dandelion grounds
   ¼ cup dandelion roots, *Taraxacum officinale,* rinsed and chopped

1. Roast dandelion roots in oven at 350°F until you smell chocolate chip cookies.

2. Remove roots from oven and put them in a grinder. Use it.

Part Two: Make Margot's Spice Mix
   3 tablespoons cinnamon
   1 teaspoon clove
   1 teaspoon allspice
   1 teaspoon or 1 large pod anise, ground
   ¾ teaspoon cardamom
   1 dash chipotle chili powder
   Optional: Ground ginger and nutmeg to taste

Combine spices in a jar.

Part Three: *Make Margot's Dandelion Spice Coffee*

    3 tablespoons pre-roasted and ground dandelion roots

    12 tablespoons roasted espresso beans

    1 tablespoon Margot's Spice Mix

    ½ teaspoon almond, vanilla, or orange extract

    Agave, brown sugar, or other sweetener to taste

    Sweetened condensed milk, coconut cream, or hemp milk to taste

1. Combine espresso beans with pre-roasted and ground dandelion root and spice mix prior to grinding.

2. Brew coffee via French press or other method.

3. Once brewed, add extract, sweetener, and cream of choice.

WILD GIRL'S NUMBER ONE BEST SUPER RELAX HAPPY TIME SMOKE MIX

Mullein leaves, *Verbascum thapsus,* dried

Lemon balm leaves, *Melissa officinalis,* dried

Russian sage flowers, *Perovskia atriplicifolia,* dried

Vanilla leaf, *Achlys triphylla,* dried

1. Dry plant materials by hanging upside down or laying them out on a screen with ventilation for several days.

2. Crumble plants by hand.

3. Mix 1 part mullein to 1 part lemon balm.

4. Add ½ part Russian sage and ½ part vanilla leaf.

5. Roll it, smoke it, and experience feel-goodness.

GREG MONZEL'S TIPI SMOKE MIX

This produces a sweet and bitter smoke with a hint of menthol. "This blend is a reasonable lung tonic with some relaxing, nervine qualities," Greg says. Lobelia is mildly uplifting and can make you feel a little bit lightheaded. It is a popular choice among cigarette smokers looking to wean themselves of the tobacco habit, because lobelia contains an alkaloid called lobeline, which is similar to nicotine but weaker.

Red clover blossoms, *Trifolium pratense*, dried
Mullein leaves, *Verbascum thapsus*, dried
Blue vervain leaves, *Verbena hastata*, dried
Lobelia leaves, *Lobelia inflata*, dried
Peppermint leaves, *Mentha piperita*, dried

1. Mix red clover blossoms and mullein leaves in equal parts.

2. Sprinkle blue vervain, lobelia, and peppermint leaves on top.

3. Roll, smoke, and enjoy.

Greg Monzel is the first herbalist I ever encountered, and I include his recipe here because he played a major role in inspiring me to learn about plants. I remember the night we first met. It was 2007. After six hours of driving north and west on winding country roads in the mountains to get to Ithaca, New York, my headlights shone on the sign for Turtle Dreams, a bed-and-breakfast with a small organic farm. I had found the place in a directory for work-trade opportunities on organic farms. The ad described it as "six acres of cosmic grooviness overlooking Fall Creek" and boasted "way yummy food for veggies and non-veggies." I was a vegetarian, so this sounded good. I'd have to garden for a few hours per day, and in exchange, I would get free room and board.

I was looking forward to this vacation. I had been working as a reporter for a daily newspaper in New Jersey, where I spent long days covering school budgets and bank robberies in a gray cubicle under fluorescent lights.

The tipi was two stories tall and wrapped in a thick, white canvas. When I stepped through the doorway, I startled the person who was about to be my roommate, a lean, bespectacled, bearded young guy around my age. He was tending a bright fire at the center of the tipi, poking at crumpled newspaper and thick logs with a long stick.

"I'm Greg," he said. "Nice to meet you."

As I unrolled my sleeping bag on the hard wooden floor, Greg told me he'd been living in the tipi for a couple of months already while attending the Northeast School of

Botanical Medicine. He said he was an herbalist and that he was especially interested in Ayurveda, traditional Indian plant medicine.

"What is herbalism?" I asked.

"Herbalism is a way of life, and also a system of health and healing using plant medicines," he told me.

"How did you get into it?" I asked.

"My father and grandfather hunted, fished, gardened, and ate wild edibles. It was something that resonated with me, and I wanted to learn how to sustain myself in the natural world much as wild animals do by thinking about what a wild human would do. And I want to help people. I feel like it's something spiritual for me," he said.

As he spoke, Greg rolled a cigarette made of plants he had picked and dried himself. I'd never seen anyone smoke anything except tobacco or marijuana before. He said the mixture of red clover, *Trifolium pratense,* and blue vervain, *Verbena hastata,* was calming. He lit it and exhaled, and a bittersweet aroma floated through the air. I watched the smoke float out through a hole in the center of the tipi above the fire.

In the soft glow I could see an animal slinking up on Greg's blanket. This, he told me, was his dearest friend, a striped feline named Kit Kat, a savvy hunter who brought his human companion gifts of bloody mice.

"Aw, it's so kind of him," Greg mused. "I feel like I should eat them."

We spent evenings walking the grounds under the moonlight and hanging out in an old trailer Greg had turned into an apothecary. He adorned the wood-paneled shelves with drying herbs he gathered from local woods and meadows: wild cherry bark, a cough remedy; *Lobelia inflata,* an anti-asthma treatment; and bundles of mugwort, *Artemisia vulgaris,* a digestive stimulant with many other uses, such as bringing on delayed menstruation. His work struck me as mysterious, powerful, and esoteric, and I admired how deeply he understood the natural world.

The parking lot of the newspaper where I worked was sandwiched between a garbage dump and a busy highway, so that when the wind rolled from the west it smelled like trash and when it blew from the east it smelled like diesel. When I returned from Turtle Dreams, I noticed there was a row of trees in the distance and I knew nothing about them. I didn't know what they were called, if the bark might be medicinal, or if the leaves were edible. I did know that the air here stunk.

I nudged some pebbles across the pavement with my shoe and weighed the pros and cons of quitting. I knew it was reckless to leave, and yet the world I saw at Turtle Dreams pulled at me like a magnet. "I don't know, Lerner," said a coworker, a serious journalist in his forties. Papers were collapsing across the country and the industry was hemorrhaging jobs by the minute. I was lucky to be a reporter at all, and if I left, there was no guarantee I would get another chance. He took a drag on his cigarette and looked at me sideways. "It's your decision," he said, shaking his head.

I couldn't help but notice that the so-called real world seemed more like a shoddy imposter. I imagined telephone wires spanning New Jersey like a giant cobweb, their wispy fibers crisscrossing a forgotten world pulsing with life and truth. I wanted to know the real "real world."

I moved into that tipi in the fall that year and enrolled in a nine-month wilderness survival skills program called Primitive Pursuits. I'm so glad I did.

WILD GIRL'S INSOMNIA SMOKE BLEND

Valerian root, *Valeriana officinalis,* dried and chopped finely

or

Passionflower leaf and flower, *Passiflora incarnata,* dried and crumbled by hand

and

Mullein leaf, *Verbascum thapsus,* dried and crumbled by hand

1. Mix the herbs together by hand.

2. Smoke them in a pipe.

Warning: Only smoke valerian if you have insomnia because it is going to knock you out and render you incapable of doing much beyond lying there. The passionflower is a better choice if you're just looking to unwind. Passionflower is also great for assuaging irritability and getting into a meditative trance.

WILD GIRL'S STINGING NETTLE PESTO

½ cup olive oil
5 large cloves garlic, chopped
2½ cups stinging nettle leaves and stems from top of plant, rinsed
½ cup Bragg's nutritional yeast
½ cup almonds
Splash water

1. Blend all ingredients in a food processor or sturdy blender.

2. Enjoy pesto as a pasta sauce, in an omelet, in a sandwich, etc.

Warning: Be careful handling the nettle—the plants retain their sting until pulverized, dried, or boiled.

WILD GIRL'S STINGING NETTLE QUICHE

½ onion, finely chopped
2 tablespoons olive oil
4 cups stinging nettle greens, *Urtica dioica,* chopped
1 piecrust, store-bought or made in advance
½ cup nutritional yeast or shredded cheese, or more to taste
1 cup nut milk
3 eggs

1. Sauté onions in olive oil until onions are soft and golden.

2. Add stinging nettle to onions, add more oil if needed, and sauté until wilted.

3. Pour mixture into bottom of piecrust.

4. Top greens with a layer of cheese, cheese substitute, or nutritional yeast.

5. Whisk nut milk with eggs, then pour on top of the greens and cheese.

6. Bake quiche in the oven for 40 minutes at 375°F.

7. Enjoy.

THANKSGIVING ROSE HIPS SAUCE
Makes 2 cups
   2 cups rose hips, de-seeded, sliced, and rinsed
   1 cup water

Supplies:
   Saucepan, stovetop, wooden spoon

1. Combine ingredients in saucepan.

2. Bring to boil.

3. Lower heat to a simmer and stir occasionally until the rose hips are a mushy sauce or paste. You may need to add a few splashes of water along the way. This part may take 20 to 30 minutes.

WILD GIRL'S GET WELL OVERNIGHT TEA

   Lemon balm leaves, *Melissa officinalis,* dried
   Rosemary leaves, *Rosmarinus officinalis,* dried
   1–2 tablespoons honey
   1 fresh lemon, halved
   1–2 droppersful Oregon grape root tincture, *Mahonia aqui-folium,* homemade or store-bought (optional)

1. Crush dry plant matter and put in a tea ball.

2. Steep in hot water until water is dark and smells strongly of the plants.

3. Add honey.

4. Squeeze fresh lemon juice into tea.

5. Optional: Add Oregon grape root tincture.

6. Drink and feel better.

WILD GIRL'S ACORN & CHESTNUT FLOUR MUFFINS STUFFED WITH ROSE HIPS

Makes 7 large muffins
   1 cup acorn flour
   1 cup chestnut flour
   4 teaspoons baking powder
   4 teaspoons cinnamon

½ teaspoon salt

½ cup brown sugar

1 cup butter or butter substitute, melted

1 cup nut milk

1 egg

1 handful rose hips, sliced, rinsed, de-seeded

Supplies:

Two mixing bowls, two mixing spoons, muffin tin, spoon, oven

1. Combine dry ingredients in one bowl.

2. Mix wet ingredients together very gently with a wooden spoon.

3. Gently stir all ingredients together, including the rose hips, making sure you do not overmix it.

4. Line or grease your muffin tin.

5. Use spoon to transfer mixture into muffin tin.

6. Bake in oven at 400°F for 15 to 20 minutes. They are ready when the top of the muffin, when touched, bounces back instead of denting.

7. Optional: When muffins are cool, top with a dollop of rose hips sauce.

Wild Girl's Blackberry Syrup

Makes 2 cups

   1½ cups brown sugar, or other sweetener of choice

   2 cups blackberries

   1 cup water

1. Combine ingredients in a saucepan over medium-high heat, stirring occasionally.

2. When mixture boils, reduce heat to medium-low and simmer 5 minutes while gently crushing blackberries using a spoon or potato masher.

3. Reduce until syrup reaches desired viscosity.

4. Remove from heat and let steep 15 minutes.

5. Strain through a mesh screen and into clean container.

6. Enjoy on pancakes, add to oil and vinegar to make a salad dressing, add to carbonated water, etc.

Appendix B: Tips for Urban Foragers

1. The best way to learn how to identify edible and medicinal plants is by seeing them in person with a knowledgeable guide who can tell you what the plants are called. These kinds of walks are offered by nature educators and park rangers at state and local parks, by herbal medicine schools, by wilderness skills schools and at primitive skills gatherings, and by experienced foragers, who are proliferating.

2. Another great way to learn about wild plants for food and medicine is to go online. There are a number of knowledgeable foragers with good blogs and YouTube videos. Here are some of my favorites:

    *   www.FirstWays.com; my blog, a free field guide and how-to to hundreds of common wild plants of the city, based in Portland

    *   www.EatTheWeeds.com; a wonderful source of plant info by wild food expert Green Deane in Florida

    *   www.HuntGatherCook.com; a foodie blog with recipes by hunter and forager-author Hank Shaw in California

    *   http://Fat-of-the-Land.blogspot.com; a lovely blog by coastal forager-author Langdon Cook in Seattle

    *   www.WildFoodGirl.com; a fun-to-read blog by Erica Marciniec in Colorado

- www.UrbanOutdoorSkills.com; a blog by culinary adventurer Pascal Baudar in Los Angeles

- www.WildManWildFood.com; a website by Fergus Drennan, a foraging expert in the United Kingdom

- http://Plants.USDA.gov; a government website with a wealth of information on the distribution and edibility of almost every plant you can think of

3. Books are very useful, too. (See *Further Reading.*)

4. Avoid collecting plants near railroad tracks and highway roadsides because both are frequently sprayed with pesticides. (Meanwhile, consider asking your local government to stop spraying them.) Better options would be parks, forests, yards, sidewalks, parking strips, open lots, school campuses, alleys, community gardens, stream banks, trails, and abandoned properties.

5. In the interest of sustainability, harvesting etiquette is to take 10 percent or less of a given stand of plants, particularly if the species is scarce where you are. However, when harvesting a "weed" or so-called undesirable species, it is usually acceptable to take an unlimited quantity. To find out whether a species is threatened, visit www.RedList.org and www.UnitedPlantSavers.org

Further Reading

Books

Ames, Kenneth M., and Maschner, Herbert D.G. *Peoples of the Northwest Coast: Their Archaeology and Prehistory*. London: Thames & Hudson, 2000.

Brill, "Wildman" Steve and Dean, Evelyn. *Edible and Medicinal Plants in Wild (and Not So Wild) Places*. New York: HarperCollins, 1994.

Buhner, Stephen Harrod. *Sacred and Herbal Healing Beers: The Secrets of Ancient Fermentation*. Boulder: Siris Books, 1998.

———. *The Secret Teaching of Plants: The Intelligence of the Heart in the Direct Perception of Nature*. Rochester, Vermont: Bear & Company, 2004.

Carson, David. *Crossing Into Medicine Country: A Journey in Native American Healing*. New York: Arcade Publishing, 2005.

Carson, Rachel. *Silent Spring*. New York: Houghton Mifflin, 1962.

Chamovitz, Daniel. *What a Plant Knows: A Field Guide to the Senses*. New York: Farrar, Straus, and Giroux, 2012.

Deur, Doug, and Turner, Nancy. *Keeping It Living: Traditions of Plant Use on the Northwest Coast*. Seattle: University of Washington Press, 2006.

Diamond, Jared. *Guns, Germs, and Steel: The Fates of Human Societies*. New York and London: W.W. Norton & Company, 1999.

Duffin, Jacalyn. *History of Medicine: A Scandalously Short Introduction*. Toronto: University of Toronto Press, 1999.

Elpel, Thomas J. *Botany in a Day: The Patterns Method of Plant Identification*. Pony, Montana: HOPS Press, 2004.

Evans, Clinton L. *The War on Weeds in the Prairie West: An Environmental History*. Calgary: University of Calgary Press, 2002.

Geniusz, Wendy Makoons. *Our Knowledge Is Not Primitive: Decolonizing Botanical Anishanaabe Teachings*. Syracuse: Syracuse University Press, 2009.

Green, James. *The Herbal Medicine-Maker's Handbook: A Home Manual*. Berkeley: Crossing Press, 2000.

Hoffman, David. *Medical Herbalism: The Science and Practice of Herbal Medicine*. Rochester, Vermont: Healing Arts Press, 2003.

Hunn, Eugene. *Nch'i-Wana, 'The Big River': Mid-Columbia Indians and Their Land*. Seattle: University of Washington Press, 1991.

Huxley, Anthony. *Plant and Planet*. New York: Viking Press, 1974.

Jones, Pamela. *Just Weeds: History, Myths, and Uses*. New York: Prentice Hall Press, 1991.

Kallas, John. *Edible Wild Plants: Wild Foods from Dirt to Plate*. Layton, Utah: Gibbs Smith, 2010.

Kelly, Robert L. *The Foraging Spectrum: Diversity in Hunter-Gatherer Lifeways*. Washington: Smithsonian Institute Press, 1995.

Moerman, Daniel E. *Native American Ethnobotany*. Portland, Oregon: Timber Press, 1998.

Moore, Michael. *Medicinal Plants of the Pacific West*. Santa Fe: Museum of New Mexico Press, 1993.

Pinchbeck, Daniel. *Breaking Open the Head: A Psychedelic Journey into the Heart of Contemporary Shamanism*. New York: Broadway Books, 2002.

Pojar, Jim, and MacKinnon, Andy. *Plants of the Pacific Northwest Coast: Washington, Oregon, British Columbia & Alaska*. Vancouver: B.C. Ministry of Forests and Lone Pine Publishing, 1994.

Thayer, Samuel. *The Forager's Harvest: A Guide to Identifying, Harvesting, and Preparing Edible Wild Plants*. Birchwood, Wisconsin: Forager's Harvest Press, 2006.

Thayer, Samuel. *Nature's Garden: A Guide to Identifying, Harvesting, and Preparing Edible Wild Plants*. Birchwood, Wisconsin: Forager's Harvest Press, 2010.

Tilford, Gregory L. *Edible and Medicinal Plants of the West*. Missoula: Mountain Press, 1997.

———. *From Earth to Herbalist: An Earth-Conscious Guide to Medicinal Plants*. Missoula: Mountain Press, 1998.

———. and Wulff, Mary L. *Herbs for Pets*. Irvine: Bowtie Press, 2009.

Turner, Nancy. *Food Plants of Coastal First Peoples*. Victoria, Canada: Royal BC Museum, 1995.

Weisman, Alan. *The World Without Us*. New York: Picador, 2007.

Wood, Matthew. *The Practice of Traditional Western Herbalism: Basic Doctrine, Energetics, and Classification*. Berkeley: North Atlantic Books, 2004.

Articles

Ames, K.M, C.M. Smith and W.L. Cornett. "Archaeological Investigations (1991–1996) at 45Cl1 (Cathlapotle), Clark County, Washington: Wapato Valley Archaeology Project Report #3." Portland State University & U.S. Fish and Wildlife Service, 1996.

Arnold, Carrie. "Are All Invasive Species Bad? Nonnative Species Unfairly Get a Bad Rap According to a New Study." *U.S. News & World Report* (online) via *Inside Science News Service*, August 31, 2011.

Arora, David. "California Porcini: Three New Taxa, Observations on Their Harvest, and the Tragedy of No Commons." *Economic Botany*, vol. 62, 2008, pp. 356–75.

Balick, M.; Kronenberg, F.; Ososki, A.L.; Reiff, M.; Fugh-Berman, A.; O'Connor, B.; Roble, M.; Lohr, P.; Atha, D. "Medicinal Plants Used by Latino Healers for Women's Health Conditions in New York City." *Economic Botany*, *vol.* 54, no. 3, 2000, pp. 344–57.

Burdick, Alan. "The Truth About Invasive Species: How to Stop Worrying and Learn to Love Ecological Intruders." *Discover Magazine*, May 2005.

Burne, Jerome. "Animal Instinct." *The Guardian*, January 17, 2002.

Cordain, Loren; Miller, Janette Brand; Eaton, S. Boyd; Mann, Neil; Holt, Susanne H.A.; and Speth, John D. "Plant-animal subsistence ratios and macronutrient energy estimations in worldwide hunter-gatherer diets." *American Journal of Clinical Nutrition*, vol. 71, 2000, pp. 682–92.

Cueterick, M.I.V.; Torry, B.; Pieroni, A. "Cross-cultural Adaptation in Urban Ethnobotany: The Colombian Folk Pharmacopoeia in London." *Journal of Ethnopharmacology*, vol. 120, 2008, pp. 342–59.

Donovan, G.H.; Butry, D.T. "Trees in the City: Valuing Street Trees in Portland, Oregon." *Landscape and Urban Planning*, vol. 94, 2010, pp. 77–83.

——. Prestemon, J.P. "The Effect of Trees on Crime in Portland, Oregon." *Environment and Behavior*, vol. 44, January 2012, pp. 3–30. Published first online, October 2010.

Eaton, S.B., Konner, M., and Shostak, M. "Stone Agers in the Fast Lane: Chronic Degenerative Diseases in Evolutionary Perspective." *American Journal of Medicine*, vol. 84, 1988, pp. 739–49.

Falck, Zachary J.S. "Controlling the Weed Nuisance in Turn-of-the-Century American Cities." *Environmental History*, vol. 7, October 2002, pp. 611–31.

Gobster, Paul H. "Urban Park Restoration and the 'Museumification' of Nature." *Nature and Culture*, vol. 2, Autumn 2007, pp. 95–114.

Heil, Martin, and Karban, Richard. "Explaining Evolution of Plant Communication by Airborne Signals." *Trends in Ecology and Evolution*, vol. 25, March 2010, pp. 137–44.

Heynan, N.C. "The Scalar Production of Injustice Within the Urban Forest." *Antipode*, vol. 35, 2003, pp. 980–98.

Hull, R.B.I. "Brief Encounters with Urban Forests Produce Moods that Matter." *Journal of Arboriculture*, vol. 18, no. 6, 1992, pp. 322–24.

Karban, Richard. "Plant Behaviour and Communication." *Ecology Letters*, vol. 11, July 2008, pp. 727–39.

Kuo, F.E.; and Sullivan, W.C. "Environment and Crime in the Inner City: Does Vegetation Reduce Crime?" *Environment and Behavior*, vol. 33, no. 3, 2001, pp. 346–67.

Larson, Brendon M.H. "The War of the Roses: Demilitarizing Invasion Biology." *Frontiers in Ecology and the Environment*, vol. 3, November 2005, pp. 495–500.

Marder, Michael. "If Peas Can Talk, Should We Eat Them?" *New York Times*, April 28, 2012.

McLain, Rebecca J. "Constructing a Wild Mushroom Panopticon: The Extension of Nation-State Control over the Forest Understory in Oregon, USA." *Economic Botany*, vol. 62, 2008, pp. 343–55.

McLain, R.J.; MacFarland, K.; Brody, L.; Hebert, J.; Hurley, P.; Poe, M.; Buttolph, L.P.; Gabriel, N.; Dzuna, M.; Emery, M.R.; and Charnley, S. "Gathering in the City: An Annotated Bibliography and Review of the Literature about Human-Plant Interactions in Urban Ecosystems." Portland, OR; U.S. Department of Agriculture, Forest Service, Pacific Northwest Research Station. www.fs.fed.us/pnw/pubs/pnw_gtr849.pdf.

McPherson, E.G.; Simpson, J.R.; Xiao, Q.; Wu, C. "Los Angeles 1-Million Tree Canopy Cover Assessment." Gen. Tech. Rep. PSW-GTR-207. Albany, CA: U.S. Department of Agriculture, Forest Service, Pacific Southwest Research Station, 2008.

Nowack, D.J.; Hoehn, R.E.I.; Crane, D.E.; Stevens, J.C.; Walton, J.T. "Assessing Urban Forest Effects and Values: Minneapolis' Urban Forest." Res. Bull. NE-166. Newton Square, PA: U.S. Department of Agriculture, Forest Service, Northeastern Research Station. 2006.

Oregon Health Authority: Public Health—Office of Environmental Public Health. "Descriptive Analsysis of PEST Cases, 2002-2007." Final report, February 22, 2010. http://public.health.oregon.gov/HealthyEnvironments/ HealthyNeighborhoods/HealthyHomes/Pesticides/ Documents/Final_Descriptive_Analysis_2002-07.pdf.

Roach, Mary. "Almost Human: The Fongoli Chimps of Senegal." *National Geographic*, April 2008.

Robbins, Paul, and Sharp, Julie T. "Producing and Consuming Chemicals: The Moral Economy of the American Lawn." *Economic Geography*, vol. 79, 2003, pp. 425–51.

Salak, Kira. "Hell and Back." *National Geographic Adventure*, March 2006.

Song Y.Y., Zeng R.S., Xu J.F., Li J., Shen X., et al. "Interplant Communication of Tomato Plants through Underground Common Mycorrhizal Networks." *PLOS ONE*, vol. 5, October 2010, e13324. www.ncbi.nlm.nih. gov/pmc/articles/PMC2954164/.

Thoreau, Henry David. "The Succession of Forest Trees." An address read to Middlesex Agricultural Society in Concord, Massachusetts, September 1860.

Tuhus-Dubrow, Rebecca. "Don't Sweat the Invasion: Why Foreign Plants and Animals May Not Be That Bad." *Slate. com*, November 4, 2009.

Turner, Allison Houlihan. "Urban Agriculture and Soil Contamination: An Introduction to Urban Gardening." University of Louisville Center for Environmental Policy and Management. Practice Guide #25, Winter 2009. http://cepm.louisville.edu/Pubs_WPapers/practiceguides/PG25.pdf.

Ulrich, R. "View Through a Window May Influence Recovery from Surgery." *Science*, vol. 224, April 1984, pp. 420–21.

United States Environmental Protection Agency: Office of Superfund Remediation and Technology Innovation. "Reusing Potentially Contaminated Landscapes: Growing Gardens in Urban Soils." Spring 2011. www .clu-in.org/download/misc/urban_gardening_fact_ sheet.pdf.

Zakay-Rones, Z.; Thom E.; Wollan, T.; Wadstein, J. "Randomized Study of the Efficacy and Safety of Oral Elderberry Extract in the Treatment of Influenza A and B Virus Infections." *The Journal of International Medical Research*, vol. 32, March/April 2004, pp. 132–40.

Index

Acknowledgments

This book would not exist without the insight, encourage-ment, and support provided by Sheila, Marshall, and Abby Lerner; Jeanette Hieter; Matt Jumago; Greg Monzel; Laurie Anne Agnese; Todd Silverstein; Joseph Hurka; Margot Berlin; Olivia Mackintosh; Jon Howells; Jodee Chizever; Leanne Smith; Marisa Novello; Magin LaSov Gregg; Lauren Sallinger; Matthew Bennett; the Turtle Dreamers; Katia "Tron" Pouleva; and Jen Jones.

Thank you to Jane Dystel, my literary agent, and to Mary Norris at Lyons Press, for believing in me as a first-time author.

Thank you to my mentors and colleagues in the creative nonfiction writing MFA program at Goucher College for their guidance in the development of the first draft of this book, especially Diana Hume George, Tom French, Laura Wexler, Mike Sager, and Patsy Sims.

For graciously and generously helping me reach accu-rate understanding in their areas of expertise, thanks are due to: Professor Valerie Hardcastle, editor of the *Journal of Consciousness Studies* and dean of McMicken College of Arts and Sciences at the University of Cincinnati, where she spe-cializes in cognitive neuroscience and philosophy of mind; Professor Anthony Trewavas at the Institute of Molecular Plant Science at the University of Edinburgh, FRS, FRSE; Professor Anurag Agrawal in the Department of Ecology and Evolutionary Biology at Cornell University; Professor Mark A. Davis, chairman of the biology department at Macalester College in St. Paul, Minnesota; Dr. Elizabeth Von Volkenburgh of the Society for Plant Signaling and Behavior, and the biology department at University of Washington; Carol C. Norton, assistant director of the Environmental Finance Center at the Center for Environmental Policy and Management at University of Louisville; Dr. Rebecca McLain of the Institute for Culture and Ecology; Dr. David G. Lewis, Tribal Museum Curator and Cultural Liaison for the Confederated Tribes of the Grand Ronde Community of Oregon; Cameron McPherson Smith, archaeologist at Portland State University; and Jenn Bildersee at the City of Portland. Thanks also to David Carson for introducing me to the Native American concept of coyote medicine.

Thanks to Jan Lundberg of Culture Change for daring me to survive on wild foods in the city and Tony Deis of TrackersEarth for helping with the wapato harvest.

Last but not least, thanks to Petunia, the best dog a writer could ever ask for.

About the Author

Rebecca Lerner, who goes by "Becky," lives in Portland, Oregon. Her web site is FirstWays.com. She has a master's of fine arts in creative nonfiction writing from Goucher College, and a bachelor's degree in philosophy from Rutgers University.

For fun, Becky enjoys playing in the woods at the end of the world, expanding her consciousness, and hanging out with the best dog in the universe, Petunia.

She works as an independent nature educator and healer, among other pursuits.